Symbols of
Power

WITHDRAWN

Symbols of
Power

Ten Coins That Changed the World

Editor
Thomas Hockenhull

Authors
Robert Bracey
Barrie Cook
Amelia Dowler
Paramdip Khera
Helen Wang

Columbia University Press
New York

Columbia University Press
Publishers since 1893
New York   Chichester, West Sussex
cup.columbia.edu

First published in 2015 by The British Museum Press
A division of The British Museum Company Ltd

ISBN: 978-0-231-17408-4 (pbk. : alk. paper)

Library of Congress Control Number: 2014955964

∞

Columbia University Press books are printed on permanent and
durable acid-free paper. This book is printed on paper with recycled
content.
Printed in China

p 10 9 8 7 6 5 4 3 2 1

Book and cover design: Bobby Birchall, Bobby&Co.
Front cover: For details of coins, see pages 21, 25, 43, 52, 70, 77, 92,
104, 124 and 138.
Frontispiece: Gold sovereign of Henry VII minted in London, 1504–9.
14.90 g, diam. 41 mm.
Above: Silver rupee of George V, 1911. 11.69 g, diam. 30 mm.
Page 6: Silver denarius minted in Rome, shortly before Julius Caesar's
murder on the Ides (15th) of March, 44 BC. 3.64 g, diam. 21 mm.

Contents

Acknowledgements

This book could not have been written without the generous
support and advice of a number of our colleagues past and
present at the British Museum, including Richard Abdy,
Benjamin Alsop, Andrew Burnett, Rupert Chapman,
Timothy Clark, Joe Cribb, Vesta Curtis, Alfred Haft,
Richard Kelleher, Ian Leins, Nicole Rousmaniere,
Christopher Stewart, Jonathan Tubb, Gareth Williams
and Jonathan Williams. We are especially indebted to
Philip Attwood, Keeper of Coins and Medals, for his
general comments about the text.

At British Museum Press we are grateful to our editor
Alice White and also to Emma Poulter and Rosemary Bradley,
for their helpful suggestions and encouragement.

Beyond the British Museum we would like to thank, for
giving up their valuable time to offer their expert opinions
about chapters in the book, Michael Bourdaghs at EALC,
University of Chicago; and Kent Deng, Leigh Gardner
and Monika Šusteková at London School of Economics.

Finally the photography, which plays such a crucial
role in bringing the narrative to life, was provided by
David Agar, Stephen Dodd, Ivor Kerslake, Saul Peckham
and John Williams.

Introduction

So much of barbarism...still remains in the transactions
of most civilized nations, that almost all independent
countries choose to assert their nationality by having,
to their own inconvenience and that of their
neighbours, a peculiar currency of their own.

John Stuart Mill (1806–73), philosopher and political economist, 1848.

WHEN EUROPEAN LEADERS met in Madrid in December
1995 to choose a name for the new single currency they might
have found these words of J.S. Mill pertinent. Suggestions for
the new name included florin, franken, ducat or écu; or even
the addition of euro as a prefix to existing currencies to create
a euromark, for example. But the politicians understood that
these terms would always be associated with individual nations,
perhaps wrongly implying that the new single currency was
based on an unequal partnership. They eventually agreed,
rather obviously in retrospect, to call it the euro, derived from
the Greek name of the mythological princess Europa and,
of course, the name of the westernmost part of the Eurasian
landmass. The euro had never been used as a monetary term
before and its introduction signified a new beginning. By giving
up their historic currencies, Europe's leaders had adopted a
name as yet unburdened by political or cultural symbolism, but
the whole process had demonstrated the continued importance
of monetary terms to concepts of cultural and political identity.

Every aspect of the design of the euro has been carefully
managed to appear politically and economically inclusive to
all its issuing countries. Even the € symbol was drawn up in
meticulous detail. It is a Greek letter epsilon, ε, and instead
of having the usual single bar added, for example the way
in which the S is barred to form the $ symbol, it has two,

running parallel. These bars are deliberately positioned in this way to suggest the stability of the currency. The coins show a map of Europe on one side, which is common for all countries. Member states then create their own designs for the other side. This continues to provide a challenge for the European Commission, which has to mediate between member states about new designs. The most problematic often involve religious imagery: in multi-faith Europe, the representation of a single religious group on circulating currency can be sensitive. Meanwhile, the notes depict historic yet non-geographically specific European architectural features, as well as a map of Europe. Unlike the coins no variation is permitted in the design: the notes circulate as foreign exchange currency and it would be too confusing to have more than one design.

This book takes ten familiar coin names and, by examining their histories, it seeks to uncover just how they became so symbolically important. The names are well known, even to

Five euro note issued by the European Central Bank, 2002. 120 x 62 mm.

those who have never used them as coins or come into direct contact with them as currencies. Some have ceased to exist as usable money, but live on in memory, language and culture. They have very diverse origins and came into existence for different reasons. The shekel, drachma, pound and mark were originally used to express weight before crossing over to express monetary value. Indeed, the terms shekel and drachma predate the use of coined money, which is thought to have been invented during the seventh century BC. The denarius and franc started out as the names of specific coins, but over time the words have been used for many different coins and units of money. Yen and rupee were both originally descriptive words that became associated with the physical appearance of coined money (yen, for example, means 'round'). Finally, the florin and the dollar are named after places, florin from Florence, Italy, and dollar an adaptation of Joachimsthaler. Joachimsthal, modern Jáchymov, a town in Bohemia, was a major source of silver in the sixteenth century AD. The coins it produced were called thalers, later anglicized to dollar.

Monetary terms, and the exchange systems they embody, have a symbolic value that often outweighs the laws of economics. Those who devise monetary policy need to understand this, said Nobel Prize winning economist Robert Mundell (1932–). His pioneering 1961 paper on 'optimum currency areas' states: 'in the real world, currencies are mainly an expression of national sovereignty, so that actual currency reorganization would be feasible only if it were accompanied by profound political changes.' This book highlights many instances where political considerations overrode monetary expedience. Israeli finance minister Yoram Aridor (1933–) was forced to resign in 1983 after suggesting that Israel should stabilize the sheqel, which had suffered high inflation, by pegging it to the US dollar. Aridor's plan was vehemently opposed by the Knesset, Israel's parliament; energy minister Yitzhak Modai (1926–1998) said 'it's like changing the flag or the anthem'. Similarly, when talking about the pound in a 1993 interview, George Carey, Archbishop of Canterbury, expressed in layman's terms the essence of Mundell's argument.

I want the Queen's head on the bank notes. The point about national identity is important.

George Carey (1935–), Archbishop of Canterbury, 1993.

In the early years of this century as questions were raised about whether Britain should join the euro, *Economic and Political Weekly* suggested that for many people the debate was not economic, but ideological: 'the pound sterling suddenly becomes not a useful currency but on a par with flag and queen and unwritten constitution, the collective essence of the British.'

These recent cases illustrate something that has been true since the earliest exchanges: people have always used money as a vehicle of symbol and meaning. Curators in the Department of Coins and Medals at the British Museum have written this book to offer a fresh look at the histories of ten coins, these 'symbols of power'. It reveals a wide range of interesting stories about where their names came from and how they evolved. From the earliest ways of measuring value to the international currencies of the twenty-first century, entire concepts of identity and belonging can be constructed around a single word.

The Shekel

*The Israeli Government today unveiled an economic
package laden with Biblical symbolism… [f]rom next
week the Israeli pound is to be replaced by a new currency
named after the Biblical shekel.*

The Times, *February 1980.*

AT ABOUT FIVE thousand years old, the shekel predates coinage.
It originated as a weight term before becoming a unit of account
for reckoning prices. Then, after coins were introduced during the
seventh century BC, it became a general term used by people to
describe silver coins that weighed a shekel. Later still it became the
official name for a coin. This chapter traces the evolution of the
shekel as a linguistic term and examines its sometimes turbulent
history, culminating in its revival as a modern currency in 1980.

The word shekel is derived from the Hebrew word for
weighing and it is known to modern audiences largely because
it features in the Hebrew books of the Old Testament of the
Bible. Yet much of what is known about the early history of the
shekel actually comes from cuneiform inscriptions on clay tablets
and inscriptions on stone found in Mesopotamia (modern Iraq)
and Iran. In the ancient Middle East a shekel weighed different
amounts according to which weight standard was being applied.
Genesis 23:16 mentions 'four hundred shekels of the standard
recognized by merchants', while Exodus 38:24 refers to a weight
standard that had been set by the temple.

Weight standards typically include a large number of
individually named subdivisions and the shekel was one of
these. In the Semitic languages of the ancient Near East people
referred to the largest weight unit as a talent, followed by the mina
and then the shekel. The relative weight of each unit differed
according to which standard was being followed. According to

The gold of the special gift used for the work of the sanctuary amounted in all to twenty-nine talents, seven hundred and thirty shekels by the sacred standard.

Exodus 38:24

Canaanite standards, for example, a talent weighed about 34.2 kilograms and a shekel weighed 11.4 grams. Yet under the Babylonian standard a shekel weighed much less, at about 8.7 grams. For anyone negotiating payments, access to a good set of weights was essential. Shekels were often measured out in multiples of two and the largest of a group of typical weights excavated at Lachish near Jerusalem weighs eight shekels according to the Judean standard. Judean weights were often made from polished limestone spheres, flattened to stand on the scales and usually engraved with their unit of weight in Egyptian hieratic script or in Hebrew. Weights could, however, be made from any material and in any shape as long as they were the correct weight. In Babylon, for example, weights were sometimes decorative as well as functional, and some were made from agate in the shape of ducks and frogs.

Although today the term 'shekel' is often associated with coins, care is needed in interpreting early references to silver measured in shekels. A reading of Genesis 37:28, for example, might give the impression that Joseph was sold into slavery for silver coins. This was not the case and the passage in fact refers to silver bullion, or unworked ingots.

Then there passed by Midianites merchantmen; and they drew and lifted up Joseph out of the pit, and sold Joseph to the Ishmaelites for twenty pieces of silver: and they brought Joseph into Egypt.

Genesis 37:28. Joseph, son of Jacob, is sold into slavery for silver.

Dome-shaped limestone eight shekel weight. Iron age, excavated at Lachish in the Levant. 91.12 g, diam. 36 mm.

The emergence of coins measured by these weight standards happened very gradually and, as the passage from Genesis infers, the first step was the adoption of silver for balancing payments, from about 2400 BC. Non-perishable materials like metals have a very long history in trade and exchange. It is clear why gold, silver and copper gained in popularity: they were not as prone to decay as perishable items such as grain, and their supply did not fluctuate seasonally. Nevertheless, grain, other foodstuffs, and items like wool continued to act as an accepted form of payment in transactions, especially for those to agricultural workers. The same weight systems were used for all these commodities and at Exodus 30:24, for instance, we read of 'five hundred shekels of cassia [beans] by the sacred standard, and a hin [about six and a half litres] of olive oil.'

A number of important inscriptions document the standardization of prices, dictating what could be bought for the value of a shekel. These law codes, proclaiming the role of the king in matters of justice, list a wide range of payments in fixed amounts of weighed silver. The Law Code of Eshnunna, for example, from the second millennium BC, gives the price of nine different commodities by weight and volume. The code lists interest rates at twenty per cent and indicates that debts could be paid in silver or grain. If the debtor had no silver then interest was valued in grain according to a silver rate. The Law Code of Eshnunna also provides a fascinating glimpse of the process for imposing fines. Financial compensation was standard in civil cases and the law codes state, for example, that someone could be fined ten shekels for slapping a person in the face. In this instance shekels of silver were being used as an accounting method, but payments or fines could be made in any material to the right value: it does not automatically mean that they were paid in silver.

Temples were an important institution within the monetary system as they stored precious metals from dedications and payments and also had the facility to provide loans. One tablet dated to 1823 BC records a loan of thirty-eight and a half shekels from the temple of the Mesopotamian god Shamash in the city of Sippar, in ancient Babylonia. The debtor, called Pururum son of

Ili-Kodari, was granted until the next harvest to repay the money he had borrowed. The loan is described as a loan from the god himself: this was standard across the ancient world for temple loans and no doubt added some incentive to repay the debt. Again, the silver loan measured in shekels should be interpreted as referring to bullion, not coins.

Pururum son of Ili-Kodari has received from the god Shamash 38½ shekels of silver. He will pay interest at the rate set by Shamash. At the time of the harvest he will repay the silver and the interest on it.

Cuneiform inscription from a clay tablet dated 1823 BC, excavated at Sippar, southern Iraq, and now at the British Museum.

It is easy to see why, for many communities accustomed to using shekel weights, the shekel would eventually become synonymous with the main unit of silver coinage: coins were, in a sense, merely weighed pieces of metal. Examples include the shekels produced by the Phoenician coastal cities of Tyre, Sidon and Byblos on a Phoenician weight standard, as well as coins struck to the Babylonian weight standard by the Persian satraps (governors) in the cities of Tarsus and Babylon.

The term shekel was also used to describe the silver coins minted by the Persian Empire, which conquered the Lydian kingdom and most of Asia Minor in 547 BC. This conquest brought the Persians into closer contact with Greeks living mainly along the western coast of Asia Minor (modern Turkey). It is likely that the Persians minted their silver coins in the old Lydian capital, Sardis. These silver coins are commonly known today as 'sigloi' because the singular, siglos, is a Greek translation of the word shekel. Large numbers of these sigloi are found in Asia Minor and it is possible that they were initially made so that the Persians could trade with coins across the Greek world. First minted under Darius I (ruled 522–486 BC) they feature a kneeling 'archer king' who holds his bow taut. A vase made in southern Italy much later, in the fourth century BC, imagines how Darius I and the royal treasurer who is seated at a table might have recorded tribute brought to him in sacks. Greek letters on the table represent values from a quarter to 10,000 shekels.

The former governors, my predecessors, had been a burden on the people, from whom they took forty shekels each day as their subsistence allowance.

Taxation could be an encumbrance, as recorded by Nehemiah, Governor of Judea under the Persian Empire, Nehemiah 5:15–18.

The Persian province of Judea, for which the shekel would later become symbolically significant, did not begin producing its own coins until the fourth century BC. However, the area had been using silver coins imported mainly from the west since the mid-sixth century and it is probable that these coins were referred to as shekels or divisions of shekels in the local Semitic languages, regardless of their original names. Lower denomination coins would have been called 'gerah' or 'ma'ah'. The Levant had many trading connections with Greek cities and other coastal regions and the designs of the first coins to be minted in the area were heavily influenced by Greek, as well as Phoenician examples. The shekels of Judea, known as the 'Yehud' coins, the Jewish name

Silver coin minted in Gaza, 5th or 4th century BC. The front of the coin shows a bearded man and the back shows the forepart of a horse, a design that was influenced by Greek coinage. 3.55 g, diam. 15 mm.

for the province, may initially have been produced at the mint of Gaza in neighbouring Philistia before production moved to Judea.

A CONTROVERSIAL COIN?

A unique quarter shekel in the British Museum features a bearded deity seated on a winged chariot, carrying a falcon on his hand. The inscription on this coin is thought to be YHD, a monogram for 'Yehud', but it could also be interpreted as 'YHW' or 'YHR', meaning 'Yahweh', or God. This is potentially controversial since the second commandment of the Hebrew Bible states 'thou shalt make no graven images of anything in heaven or on earth'. However, it is possible that the coin was initially produced at Gaza, a pagan city. If this is the case then the featured deity is only one amongst a vast pantheon of gods that existed across the Middle East at this time, and the controversy is thus averted.

Silver quarter shekel coin minted in Judea, 4th century BC. 3.29 g, diam. 15 mm.

Yehud coins continued to be produced after the victory of Alexander the Great over local Persian rule in 333 BC, but they were gradually dropped by his successors in favour of Greek coins based on a different weight standard. The Hellenistic period also witnessed a wider use of the Greek language in administration, replacing much of the Aramaic previously used under the Persians. The shekel survived as a term for silver coins in areas with a Semitic language, but the dynasties which ruled Judea from the second century BC onwards could not have produced silver shekel coins since they minted only bronze coins. Silver coins continued to be produced in Syria, Asia Minor and Phoenicia: the city of Tyre in Phoenicia, for example, continued to mint shekels until the first century AD.

Tyre was a particularly important coin producer: its coins were produced on a local weight standard and were variously described as shekels, tetradrachms or staters, the terminology depending on the language of the speaker or writer. The city had produced

Silver shekel minted in Tyre, 59 BC. 13.92 g, diam. 29 mm.

coins before, until it lost its independence to the Seleucid dynasty
who ruled a successor kingdom to Alexander the Great after
323 BC. The Seleucids ruled Tyre for almost two centuries until
about 126 or 125 BC, when the city regained its independence
and almost immediately redesigned its coins. These new shekels
looked similar to Seleucid and Ptolemaic coins since they featured
an eagle on the reverse and were inscribed in Greek. However,
the image of the king on the other side was replaced with a bust
of Melkart, the Phoenician mythical hero and equivalent of the
Greek hero Herakles.

The silver in the shekels of Tyre was purer than that of other
coins produced in the area, and so they were the coin of choice
for paying the Temple tribute obligatory for Jewish men. They
became an integral part of Jewish religious life as all Jewish males
over the age of twenty were required to pay tribute, valued at half
a shekel, each year. The solicitation of this tax forms the basis for
one of Jesus' miracles, which begins with tax collectors visiting
Jesus and the apostle Peter at Capernaum on the Sea of Galilee
to demand the payment of tribute (Matthew 17:27). They have

no money, so Jesus tells Peter to throw a line into the sea and to open the mouth of the first fish he catches. Peter duly obeys and finds a shekel (translated into 'stater' for the mainly Greek-speaking readers of the New Testament) in the mouth of the fish. This shekel would have been payment for both men. The Temple also required other payments, probably in shekels of Tyre, for the fulfilment of vows, purchase of sacrificial offerings and a five-shekel redemption price levied on firstborn males.

Take the Levites in place of all the firstborn of Israel, and the livestock of the Levites in place of their livestock. The Levites are to be mine. I am the Lord. To redeem the 273 firstborn Israelites who exceed the number of the Levites, collect five shekels for each one, according to the sanctuary shekel, which weighs twenty gerahs.

Numbers 3:45–7.

It might seem odd that shekels produced in Tyre were used as the coins for Temple tribute since they clearly depict a pagan god. The Jewish laws against both graven images and worshipping other gods are very strict, and so a coin from the pagan city of Tyre would perhaps not be the most obvious choice. However, as Jewish texts specify, it was the purity of the silver which mattered in payments to the Temple, and not the design on the coin. The silver coins of Tyre were certainly the purest in silver content in the area by a long way and so were really the only suitable candidate for Temple payments.

In addition to the half-shekel Temple tribute that was required, an additional fee had to be paid at the money changer's table, the ancient equivalent of paying commission at a currency exchange. These are the same money changers whose stalls occupied the Temple courtyard and were overturned by Jesus in the narrative about the 'cleansing of the Temple'. The purpose of the money changers was primarily to serve the people who arrived with other coins, by changing them into Tyrian shekels. Oddly enough the Talmud suggests that, even if someone showed up at the Temple with a half-shekel coin from Tyre, he would still have to pay the extra fee to sanctify the payment. Perhaps this can be explained in terms of silver content: although the coin weighed half a shekel, it did not contain half a shekel's worth of silver, since the metal contained some impurities. The payment of an extra fee would thus bring the payment up to the equivalent of a half-shekel weight in silver.

JUDAS AND THE THIRTY PIECES OF SILVER
Judas Iscariot is recorded as betraying Jesus for thirty pieces of silver, identifying him to waiting soldiers with a kiss. The Bible does not specify which silver coins were used for this payment. However, since

Tyrian shekels were widely used to pay Temple tribute, it is likely that they were the coins in question. In one version of how Judas met his end, he returned the money he had received to the priests and then hanged himself. This is often depicted in engravings of the Passion in which the bag of coins is seen beside Judas as he puts the rope around his neck and prepares to commit suicide.

Judas Iscariot seated under a tree and tying a rope around his neck, a pouch of coins lying next to it. Etching by Willem van Swanenburg (1580–1612) after Abraham Bloemaert (1564–1651), 1611. 270 x 171 mm.

Exactly when Tyre stopped producing silver shekels is unclear. However, the coins all feature a date in Greek letters following the dating system of the city of Tyre, and from this it appears that they were probably produced up until about AD 66, the outbreak of the First Jewish-Roman War, sometimes called the Great Revolt. Production appears to have stopped just as the rebels began minting their own silver coins in the first year of the revolt.

The First Jewish-Roman War, which lasted five years, transformed the shekel into a potent symbol of political defiance. Significantly, these were the first coins specifically to be marked with the denomination 'shekel'. The war was triggered by the seizure of seventeen talents from the Temple treasury by Gessius Florus, the Roman Procurator in AD 65, as well as the harsh taxation regime imposed by the Romans. During the war the rebels minted shekels, half shekels and quarter shekels in Jerusalem, dating each coin with the year of the new regime.

Shekels produced during the war served an important function in Jewish religious practice as good quality silver coins remained the form of payment required for the tribute to the Temple. Thus they are inscribed in archaized Hebrew and not Aramaic, even though Aramaic was, by the first century AD, more commonly used in spoken and written secular communication. The imagery is also strongly representative of traditional Jewish religious practice; the shekel features a chalice which probably

Silver shekel from the First Jewish-Roman War, minted in Jerusalem, AD 66–7. 14.15 g, diam. 22 mm.

represents the Omer cup, used on the second day of Passover. The cup would have contained the Omer, a measure of barley which was offered as the first fruits to the Temple. The reverse of the coin features three pomegranates which, in reference to the many seeds of the fruit, probably symbolized fertility. The number of seeds may also represent the number of laws in the Torah, the first part of the Jewish bible. The pomegranate was one of the symbols adorning the Temple and part of the decoration of the high priest's robes.

Having initially occupied the Temple Mount area of Jerusalem, the Jewish army tried to gain control of the whole city. There were initial victories for the army, particularly the capture of the Roman fortress overlooking the Dead Sea at Masada. Masada famously held out for three years after the end of the war before it was recaptured. Jerusalem however fell in AD 70 and the Temple was destroyed. Holy objects from the Temple including the showbread table and menorah were taken to Rome and placed in the Temple of Peace, as recorded on the Arch of Titus in Rome.

A second rebellion, known as the Bar Kochba Revolt after its leader, Simon bar Kochba (Simon ben Kosiba in Hebrew), took place from AD 132 to 135. Once again the Jews minted coins in silver and bronze but, unlike the coins of the first war, the silver coins do not have their denominations inscribed on them. No coins on a local weight standard were produced since the coinage was struck on silver coins already in circulation from other areas. This was because, unlike the first war when the rebels were based in Jerusalem, during the second war the rebels had no base and had to move constantly through the desert. While they were able to strike the coins using only hammers and dies, which were relatively moveable, they lacked the facility to smelt alloys and to cast blanks for striking. The silver sela coin, for example, was mainly struck over silver tetradrachms of Antioch in Syria and traces of the original designs can often be seen. The new design of the coins featured a temple to reflect the fact that the Bar Kochba Revolt had, in part, been triggered by a desire to rebuild the Temple in Jerusalem. It is not clear whether the coins were known officially as shekels but it is possible that the term was applied locally to the sela, which was similar in size and shape to the shekels of the first war. In AD 135 the rebels were finally defeated and expelled from Jerusalem by the Romans.

In coinage terms, the shekel's story might have ended here, but it received an unexpected twentieth-century revival with a law passed by the Knesset, Israel's parliament, on 4 June 1969. The law was deliberately vague but provided for the shekel, or sheqel, divided into a hundred new agorot, to replace the Israeli pound, at a date yet to be determined. Clearly the government was waiting for the most fiscally viable climate in which to replace its currency, since the Israeli pound had been experiencing high levels of inflation since the early 1960s. Inflation of the Israeli pound accelerated in the 1970s and the government was forced to act. In May 1978 Prime Minister Menachem Begin agreed to introduce the sheqel, with new notes and coins appearing in 1980. Apart from a devaluation which resulted in the cancelling of a zero from the currency, the new notes were very similar in design and colour to the old pound notes. Finance Minister Yigael Hurwitz said that, by adopting the sheqel, Israel was 'returning to its roots' and the new coins featured the Omer cup, in reference to the shekels of the First Jewish-Roman War.

The revived sheqel initially suffered the same fate as the Israeli pound, leading to Yoram Aridor's aforementioned suggestion that Israel should dollarize. Instead, the Bank of Israel replaced it with what was officially called the new sheqel in 1985. Its introduction was brought about as a result of the Economic Stabilization Plan which aimed to curb inflation by adopting a conservative fiscal policy. A strengthening of the Israeli economy in the 2000s added value to the new sheqel and it became freely convertible against other currencies in 2003. Its twentieth-century revival provides perhaps an odd coda for a term that came into existence five thousand years ago, but it reflects the shekel's multi-layered history. Beginning as a practical solution to help standardize accounting, it developed into a symbolic representation of historic continuity for the people of Israel.

The Drachma

*Athenian tetradrachms [four-drachma coins], bolstered
by the Athenian naval force, became a true international
currency. They were accepted all over the Mediterranean
world, while various imitations travelled all the way to
Persia and Arabia.*

Theodoros B. Karatzas (1930–2004), Governor of the National Bank of Greece, 2001.

WRITING IN 2001, the Governor of the National Bank
of Greece drew a direct comparison between the Athenian
tetradrachm (four-drachma) coins of classical Greece and the
euro. His comments were auspicious: Greece was in the process
of abandoning its greatly devalued modern drachma to adopt
the European single currency. This chapter examines the ancient
use of the drachma and the reasons why its modern revival was
symbolic and yet fraught with difficulty.

In ancient Greek 'drachma' means 'a handful' and its use
derives from a time when values were measured using iron
nails or 'spits' called obols. Obols were typically about ninety
centimetres long and it was said that six of them made a
drachma, a 'handful' because that was as many as a hand could
grasp. Eventually precious metals, especially silver, were adopted
for exchange against other goods and the drachma was retained
as a word describing the equivalent value in a fixed weight of
silver. Both obols and drachmas became coinage terms after coins
were introduced to Greece during the sixth century BC.

There were many drachma weight standards in the Greek
world because Greece was not one country but was made up of
rival city states which defined the weight of a drachma differently.
The standard that would have lasting impact was the Attic
standard named after the region of Attica, a peninsular on the
Greek mainland with Athens its most prominent city. According

Pheidon of Argos was the first to strike coinage on Aegina [in the seventh century BC]; and after giving out the coinage and taking in the obeliskoi (iron spits) he offered them to Hera at Argos. And since then the obeliskoi filled his hand, making a handful, we call it a drachma from drachasthai (to grasp).

'Obolos', from Orion's Etymologicum, *written about AD 1150. The passage is somewhat inaccurate and it seems unlikely that Pheidon of Argos was the first to introduce coins to Greece.*

to this standard, a drachma weighed 4.3 grams of silver. By comparison, the Corinthian standard drachma weighed 2.9 grams but mostly appeared as a three-drachma coin. Some of the weight systems were compatible, and it has been suggested that the Corinthian standard was actually designed to mediate between the Attic and Aeginetan (from the island of Aegina) standards.

Aegina, Corinth and Athens were the earliest producers of coins in Greece after coinage was introduced from Asia Minor. From these centres production gradually spread so that coinage was well established by the end of the sixth century BC. Conservative Sparta was a notable exception and is supposed to have enforced the continued use of iron spits for transactions, producing no coins at all until the third century BC. As well as producing coins on different weight standards, city states tended to favour the production of coins in different drachma fractions and multiples. The four-drachma coin, the tetradrachm, was the most common.

Athenian silver coinage, 6th–4th centuries BC (in order of size): decadrachm, 42.71 g, diam. 33 mm; tetradrachm, 17.2 g, diam. 25 mm; didrachm, 8.52 g, diam. 18 mm; drachm, 4.28 g, diam. 14 mm; hemidrachm, 2.11 g, diam. 12 mm; obol, 0.71 g, diam. 8 mm; hemiobol, 0.38 g, diam. 6 mm; tetartemorion, 0.16 g, diam. 4 mm.

SMALL CHANGE Until the fourth century BC Greek coins were minted almost exclusively in precious metals, especially silver. Small denominations were produced by reducing the weight and, accordingly, the size of the coins. This meant that the smallest subdivisions of the drachma were tiny and could be easily lost. Ancient writers wrote that to keep them somewhere safe many people resorted to storing coins in their mouths under their gums. This was once thought to be an exaggeration but small silver coins have since been found in a number of excavated latrines, suggesting that that not only did people carry coins in their mouths but also occasionally swallowed them by accident. The comic playwright Aristophanes (about 446–380 BC) based a joke in *The Wasps* on the suggestion that obols (one-sixth of a drachma) were so small they could be mistaken for fish scales.

...that damned jester, Lysistratus, played me an infamous trick the other day. He received a drachma for the two of us and went on the fish-market to get it changed and then brought me back three mullet scales. I took them for obols and crammed them into my mouth; but the smell choked me and I quickly spat them out.

An ancient latrine at Ephesus, modern Turkey.

Each city state chose a specific image for its coins to symbolize its identity. As the coins were struck by hand they were not always of uniform shape: the important point was to make sure that the weight was correct. Coins of Aegina featured a turtle because it was a sea-faring island, while a winged Pegasus appeared on coins of Corinth in reference to Bellerophon, mythical ancestor of the kings of Corinth and rider of the winged horse. The coins of Athens featured the helmeted head of Athena, goddess of war and protector of the city, with an owl on the reverse. Owls were a common sight in the ancient city and supposedly roosted in the old Parthenon. This led to the phrase 'bringing owls to Athens' to describe a pointless or superfluous undertaking.

Who to Athens brings owls?

A line from Aristophanes' play The Birds *first performed 414 BC.*
'Owls' had a double meaning, referring to both the bird and to Athenian coins.

Athenian 'owl' tetradrachms have been found in hoards in India, Egypt, Tunisia and Spain, suggesting that they were used extensively for overseas trade. There are two main reasons why they became so common in the fifth century BC. Firstly Athens was rich in silver because it operated a mine at Laurium in Attica. By minting coins with a reputation for purity it was able to export large quantities of silver. Secondly, Athens supplemented its income by being head of a league of its allies. The century had begun under perilous circumstances, with the Persian invasion of the Greek mainland. At the end of the war a number of cities and islands had good reason to remain nervous about Persia and formed the Delian League against renewed Persian aggression. However the League quickly became dominated by Athens. Since Athens supplied and maintained the defensive naval fleet, reasoned the general Pericles in 454 BC, it was entitled to move the treasury from its neutral home on the island of Delos to the Athenian Acropolis.

The tribute collected to maintain the fleet enabled Athens to supplement the minting of its 'owl' tetradrachms. On the Acropolis in Athens at the time there was an intensive programme of building activity, which no doubt required the payment of labourers, providing a further reason for the production of coins in huge numbers. Speaking in 431 BC, Pericles provided some indication of the wealth that Athens had been able to amass: '…usually six hundred talents came in annually to the city as tribute from the allies, apart from other income, and there were…on the Acropolis six thousand talents of coined silver'. To put this into perspective, 6,000 talents of coined silver was the equivalent of 9 million Athenian 'owl' tetradrachms. Athens' military and economic domination was resented by its allies, resulting in war between 431 and 404 BC.

The Peloponnesian War as it came to be known, since it involved most of the city states in central Greece, had a catastrophic impact on the Athenian coinage. This was because the mines at Laurium were closed when its slaves seized the opportunity to defect to Sparta in 413 BC. In desperation Athens turned the gold statues of Nike (Victory) from the Parthenon into coins and issued silver-plated bronze coins to pay its soldiers. The loss of the mines greatly compromised Athens' financial strength and the further loss of its allies, who no longer paid tribute, was a major factor enabling Sparta to emerge as victor in the war.

Every one of the hoplites…received two drachmas a day.

History of the Peloponnesian War *by Thucydides,*
written late fifth century BC.

Beyond the city states of central Greece, other Greek-speaking areas also used the drachma in the fifth century BC. To the north in the kingdom of Macedonia, a king called Alexander I produced coins between about 478 and 452 BC. It was said that his primary silver mine yielded a talent, or 6,000 drachmas, a day. Greek colonies in Italy and Sicily also produced drachma coins, often on the Attic standard but also on Corinthian and other local standards. The most important cities in Sicily were ruled by noblemen who set up lavish courts and behaved as if they were monarchs. They were called tyrants, although the meaning is slightly different today and they were not necessarily despotic. Gelon, tyrant of Syracuse, issued silver tetradrachms featuring a chariot crowned by Nike, goddess of Victory. The reverse shows the water nymph Arethusa surrounded by dolphins. These magnificent coins are presumed to commemorate Gelon's win in a race at the Olympics in 488 BC. By about 450 BC most of the tyrannies on Sicily had been overthrown, but the island's Greek cities continued to produce high-quality coinage. From around 415 until 400 BC Syracuse produced a fine series of coins that were sometimes signed by their engraver. Their artistry is all the more remarkable because in the same period the city suffered almost continuous invasion attempts by Athens and Carthage, and they were probably minted to supply large coins to pay soldiers. From the third century BC the growing influence of Rome began to have an impact on the coinage of the former Greek colonies in the western Mediterranean and after 300 BC Syracuse remained the only Sicilian city to issue drachmas.

Silver decadrachm of Syracuse, late 5th century BC. The signature of Kimon, its engraver, is on the dolphin below the portrait. 43.36 g, diam. 35 mm.

THE COST OF LIVING In Athens in the fourth century BC a pig's trotter, considered a delicacy, cost an Attic drachma. Or it was possible to buy three litres of wine for about one Attic drachma and four obols. By comparison, a common labourer in Eleusis in 329–328 BC could expect to earn one Athenian drachma and three obols for his daily wage. Generally speaking, the cost of living was quite low since a labourer would have his wage paid in both food and coins. A Cretan inscription from the late third century BC records a treaty providing soldiers with a daily ration of one 'choinix' (839 grams) of grain and one Aeginetan weight drachma.

Back in Greece at the start of the fourth century BC, the defeat of Athens created a power vacuum that various alliances attempted to fill, and a number of city states experienced an upsurge in coin production. As the Greek city states squabbled amongst each other, they at first barely noticed the emergence of a new power in the north, in the kingdom of Macedonia. Philip II acceded to the Macedonian throne in 359 BC and within two years he had captured gold mines at the nearby settlement of Krenides, which he enlarged and renamed Philippi after himself. They brought him annual revenue of more than a thousand talents. Previously, gold coins had only been issued as a result of war, but Philip's revenues enabled him to introduce a regular gold coinage to Greece for the first time. The coins were valued at six silver tetradrachms to one gold stater.

Philip conquered central Greece and was on the verge of invading Persia in 336 BC when he was assassinated, leaving his son Alexander III (the Great) to succeed him and continue producing coins. Alexander's silver tetradrachm coins initially followed the Chalcidian standard but he soon abandoned it in favour of the Attic standard and, even though Athens was no longer such a prominent city, its weight standard lived on because of this. Alexander's tetradrachm coins weighed the same as Athenian 'owl' tetradrachms and before long they were just as common. The coins featured the head of Herakles (the Greek for Hercules), legendary ancestor of the Macedonian royal house, wearing a lion skin on the front and a seated figure of Zeus on the

Silver tetradrachm of Alexander III (the Great), minted in Memphis, Egypt, 332–323 BC. 17.08 g, diam. 27 mm.

back. Zeus was also supposedly an ancestor of the Macedonian royal house, but his inclusion here was chosen to appeal to all Greeks, reflecting Alexander's adoption of a 'Panhellenic' position; his army, assembled for the Persian invasion, was made up of soldiers from all over Greece.

On Alexander's death in 323 BC the huge empire he had conquered was divided among his generals who initially copied the design of his tetradrachms and other coins to emphasize their legitimacy as his heirs. Gradually, however, they began to introduce their own designs. Many were in a similar style to Alexander's coin types and in some cases used direct references to Alexander, for example by portraying his now deified portrait. 'Posthumous' Alexander coins were minted in huge numbers by both Greek and non-Greek cities around the eastern Mediterranean, Aegean and Black Sea. Since they all used similar imagery and were all based upon the Attic weight standard they were used widely in trade. Alexander-type tetradrachms circulated for a long time, so long in fact that as they became worn with use their weight dropped. New coins were minted at this lower weight and, correspondingly, over the next century the weight of the Attic-standard drachma decreased by more than a gram.

In Greece coins continued to be minted, mainly on the Attic standard, but also on other local standards or on new lighter drachma standards. Coin hoards from the late fourth century BC feature a large proportion of Macedonian coins, suggesting that other states were producing fewer of their own coin types. In the third century BC a new league of cities in southern Greece called the Achaean League emerged as a major coin producer, issuing a half drachma featuring the head of Zeus. In the 220s BC even Sparta began to belatedly produce tetradrachms on the Attic standard.

TETRADRACHMS OF RHODES The island of Rhodes produced a tetradrachm after 282 BC featuring Helios, the sun god, with rays at his head instead of a halo. In the middle ages the portrait was mistaken for Jesus. Like most coins from Rhodes, the coin features a wild rose, a pun on the name of the island.

By the second century BC Rome's influence in Greek affairs had a tremendous impact on the coinage, especially when Corinth, previously a major coin producer, was completely destroyed in 146 BC. New cities began to issue coins to cope with continued demand and, as a result, a new style of Athenian 'owl' tetradrachm came to prominence. Under the Romans these new style tetradrachms effectively became the official Greek coinage and were produced in large numbers. Meanwhile, in western Europe, Emporium in Spain and Massalia in Gaul (France) remained for a while as solitary outposts of the drachma's influence, but the last drachmas beyond Greece were probably issued in Illyria, Apollonia and Dyrrhachium in the western Balkans for Roman military payments, and possibly also for regional trade in Celtic slaves.

Silver tetradrachm of Athens, minted 120–119 BC. This new style Athenian tetradrachm was inscribed with the name Aphrodisi-Dioge, who was a magistrate, or official. 16.64 g, diam. 28 mm..

PTOLEMAIC AND ROMAN EGYPT After the death of
Alexander the Great in 323 BC his trusted general Ptolemy (about
367–283 BC) took control of Egypt. He issued Attic-standard silver
tetradrachm coins for a few years but then reduced their weight,
effectively turning Egypt into a closed monetary system. By cutting
Egypt off from the wider Greek world Ptolemy ensured that the
coinage developed separately to, and was largely unaffected by,
changes to the drachma elsewhere. During the Roman period
the Egyptian port of Alexandria became an important producer of
tetradrachm coins, which remained the standard denomination until
the monetary reforms of the Roman emperor Diocletian (ruled
AD 245–311) in the late third century AD. Tetradrachms of Alexandria
bear little resemblance to the silver tetradrachms of Greece: they were
made from billon, a copper alloy with only a tiny amount of added silver.

Silver tetradrachm of Ptolemy I, minted in Egypt, late 4th century BC, at a lower
weight than the Attic standard. 14.79 g, diam. 28 mm.

The end of the ancient drachma in Greece came about as an
indirect consequence of Rome's civil wars in the first century BC.
As the Roman Republic crumbled, Greece became a battleground
where soldiers were sent to quell a series of internal struggles
between generals. A soldier's pay was measured in denarii (see
the next chapter) and portable mints were taken with the army
to pay the soldiers. The latest issues of Thessaly's tetradrachms
probably date to the 50s BC and Athenian tetradrachms ceased
to be produced in the 40s BC, although the production of bronze
coins continued. Macedonia, meanwhile, struck a number of

tetradrachms in the name of the Roman quaestor (official) Aesillas (lived early first century BC) who revived the portrait of Alexander the Great on the coins. Gradually, however, the Roman denarius took over as the main unit of silver coin. The Greek drachma continued to be used as a term for measurement, especially for fluids (as one might today, for example, drink a 'dram' of whisky).

Beyond the reaches of the Roman Empire, primarily in the Middle East, the drachma endured for longer. The first Parthian drachmas, or 'drachms', appeared in ancient Iran and Mesopotamia (modern Iraq) from around 240 BC and remained in use until about AD 224, when they were superseded by Sasanian drachms. These in turn circulated until after the Sasanian Empire was ended by Islamic conquest in AD 651. The Umayyad ruler Abd al-Malik ibn Marwan (ruled AD 685–705) began a series of wide-ranging reforms to the coinage in AH 72 in the Islamic calendar, or AD 692–3. This included the introduction of Islamic inscriptions to the silver drachms which, after AH 79 (AD 698–9), became known as a dirhams. The dirham was later adopted by other Islamic dynasties, including the Ottomans of Turkey. Today it is the currency of several Arab states that include Morocco and the United Arab Emirates.

The path to the drachma's revival as a modern currency began during the Greek war of independence against Ottoman rule, 1821–32. Greece experimented with a number of monetary systems and the one that initially looked likely to last was called the phoenix. It was introduced in 1828 by Ioannis Kapodistrias (1776–1831), the first governor of Greece. The new coins were minted, appropriately enough, on the island of Aegina where Greek coinage supposedly began, using minting equipment imported from Malta. Featuring a phoenix on their reverse, the coins were intended to symbolize the rebirth of the Greek nation from the ashes of Ottoman rule. But they were introduced during a tumultuous period that proved to be too unstable to support a silver currency and monetary reform was halted after Kapodistrias was assassinated in 1831. The phoenix had been unable to gain public confidence and so was abandoned after merely five years, when in 1833 it was decided to replace the phoenix with the drachma.

Deliberately recalling Greece's classical past, the reintroduction of the drachma demonstrated a renewal of interest in Greek history and an idealized sense of nationhood. The new drachma was placed on a bimetallic standard, in which the currency was backed by both a gold and silver reserve, with the standard unit heavier than the phoenix but lighter than the other major European currencies. To promote acceptance of the drachma the government prohibited the use of the Turkish piastre, although in practice these coins continued to circulate and, in many cases, remained the most popular form of transaction. Drachma notes followed after the founding of the National Bank of Greece in 1841. These were printed in France and issued in denominations from twenty-five to five hundred drachmas.

The reintroduced drachma was plagued by political turmoil, budget crises, state defaults and isolation from international currency markets. In 1848, for example, during the so-called 'Year of Revolution' that engulfed Europe, the price of currants, Greece's largest export, dropped. This led to a run on the reserves of the National Bank, which fell from 626,000 drachmas in February to 215,000 drachmas in March, causing convertibility from notes to coins to be temporarily suspended. Furthermore, Greece was experiencing political upheaval as a result of the long process of unification. As more islands joined the kingdom, the economic burden increased and the government found itself increasingly in debt. In 1867 government debt stood at just over 9.5 million drachmas, increasing to almost 15.8 million drachmas the following year as a consequence of a revolution on Crete. In 1869 the National Bank refused to extend further credit to the government. A panic ensued that caused a run on the bank's reserves, and the backing of banknotes with precious metal was suspended again until a compromise could be sought.

In 1868 Greece applied to join the Latin Monetary Union, Europe's first major experiment with monetary union in modern times, although its membership was not formalized until 1876. The Latin Monetary Union, which is explained in more detail in the chapter on the franc, put the drachma on a par with the currencies of France, Belgium, Italy and Switzerland. Yet Greece was always the weakest economy in this union and increasingly relied upon foreign currency to supply its monetary needs. In 1893 lack of sufficient metallic currency caused the government to default on its foreign debt payments.

Into the twentieth century, problems with the Greek monetary supply remained. Indeed, almost no coinage was issued during the reigns of Constantine I, 1913–17 and 1920–2. The new Hellenic Republic of 1925–35 issued a full drachma series of coins and in 1930 it even revived the phoenix motif from the drachma's short-lived predecessor (the phoenix would become a regular feature on drachma coins after the restoration of a monarchy in 1973). But then worldwide depression in the 1930s greatly devalued the drachma and forced Greece into a period of economic and political instability culminating in dictatorship in 1936. The situation was made worse by the German occupation in the Second World War, when the treasury was looted and the drachma experienced hyperinflation.

At the end of the war a new revalued drachma was launched solely in paper money. However, this also experienced high

Silver five drachma coin issued by the Republic of Greece, 1930. 10.1 g, diam. 30 mm.

10,000,000,000 drachma note issued by the Bank of Greece during hyperinflation of the currency in 1944. The note reproduces an image of an ancient coin of Syracuse, Sicily, depicting the water nymph Arethusa. 139 x 63 mm.

inflation until, in 1953, Greece joined the Bretton Woods fixed exchange rate system in which a number of currencies were pegged to the US dollar. The relative stability provided by Bretton Woods enabled the resumption of coin production for the first time in almost a quarter of a century. The fortunes of the drachma were ultimately tied to those of larger economies, and high inflation ensued almost immediately after Bretton Woods was finally abandoned in 1973. By the time Greece joined the euro in 2002, the exchange rate had fallen from thirty to around four hundred drachmas to the dollar.

The switch to the euro prompted few feelings of nostalgia for the abandoned drachma: the Governor of the National Bank of Greece said that the euro ushered in a 'brave new reality' and that 'a new era of monetary union, cooperation and stability in Europe' lay ahead. Designs for Greek euro coins were chosen not in reference to features of the modern drachma, but instead by delving into Greece's classical history. The one-euro coin, for instance, depicts a fifth-century BC Athenian 'owl' tetradrachm. The drachma might have ceased to exist as a monetary term, but its image endures as a result of its classical past and its continued association with Greek nationhood.

Bi-metallic euro coin issued in Greece, 2006. 7.48 g, diam. 23 mm.

The Denarius

'SILVER HAS NO COLOUR when it is hidden away in
the miserly earth', mused the poet Horace (65–8 BC). His
philosophical comment suggests silver's prominent place
in the Roman monetary system. It also provides an apt
description of the process by which their coins have survived
to the present through archaeological burial. The silver
denarius was, by the time of his writing in the turbulent years
of the later Roman Republic, the main unit of reckoning
throughout the Roman world. Its influence outlasted the
Roman Empire and set the template for the silver coinages
of medieval and modern Europe.

The denarius was launched in about 211 BC against the
financially costly backdrop of Rome's conflict with Carthage,
its main rival in the Mediterranean. This was during the
second of three wars, known as the Punic Wars, fought by
Rome against Carthage. The second Punic War (218–201 BC)
is perhaps best known for Hannibal's invasion of Italy by
crossing the Alps with an army that included elephants. War
was expensive and forced Rome to reorganize the coinage
which, before 212 BC, had been based on silver coins of
a weight standard comparable to Greek coins. Containing
around seven grams of silver, these coins had probably been
valued at two drachmas. Logically the Romans could simply
have halved the silver content of the coins to create a single
drachma that would retain compatibility with Greek coins.

However, in a bold assertion of political independence
the Romans introduced the denarius, at a weight that bore
no obvious comparison to what had gone before. Containing

about four and a half grams of silver, its name derived from the Latin for ten, because it was worth ten standard bronze coins, each known as an 'as'. This Latin word for a weight and arithmetical unit shares similar derivation to the familiar card term 'ace'. The new denarius featured the Roman numeral X behind the head of Roma to remind people of its value, ten, or a 'tenner', in relation to the as.

Just as modern coins often carry emblems encapsulating national identity and pride, the design of the denarius was intended to announce the power and might of Rome. Roma, goddess of Rome, wears a winged helmet and the reverse shows the heroic mythological twins Castor and Pollux, armed and riding horses. There was a belief that they had miraculously appeared at the battle of Lake Regillus in 499 BC to rescue the Roman army from the brink of defeat.

Victory over Carthage in 201 BC gave Rome almost unrivalled access to the whole of the western Mediterranean and there followed many centuries of imperial expansion,

Silver denarius of Rome, 211–210 BC. 4.28 g, diam. 19 mm.

THE EARLY COINS OF ITALY The denarius was introduced towards the end of the third century BC, during which Rome had begun to present a politically and culturally distinct identity on its coinage. But before recognizably Roman coinage appeared, transactions were probably carried out using crude lumps of copper, known as 'aes rude'. These lumps could easily be mistaken for by-products of copper smelting processes were it not for the frequency of their occurrence in hoards dating to the period. They developed into the larger but more formally shaped 'aes grave' (heavy bronze). These were sizeable objects and the author Livy (64 or 59 BC–AD 17) wrote about senators carrying their wealth around in ox carts.

In about 300 BC the Romans became inspired by Greek settlements in southern Italy and their sophisticated systems of weights and measures which included coins made from silver. The first Roman silver coins, forerunners of the denarius, appeared along similar Greek lines (in drachm and occasionally double drachm units) from the early third century BC. The Romans distinguished them from the coinage of their Greek neighbours by the Latin inscription 'ROMANO', probably meaning 'of the Romans'. The designs chosen had a distinct national flavour too, including a type with the badge of Rome, the she-wolf suckling the twins Romulus and Remus.

extending the influence of the denarius far beyond Italy. Merchants began to venture further afield. Existing trade networks were expanded to areas which already had flourishing cities, while new towns sprung up where Roman soldiers were garrisoned or where trading could flourish under Roman security. The Romans were not merely content to trade but wanted to take control of these hitherto inaccessible territories. Not only did the annexation of new lands introduce coins such as the denarius, it also gave the Romans access to the wealth of their new subjects. The conquest of Macedonia in 167 BC, for example, raised about 75 million denarii in booty, equivalent to about 324 metric tonnes of silver. The conquest of Egypt in 30 BC provided an even bigger windfall and prompted a huge drop in interest rates in Rome due to the plentiful supply of money.

To the soldiers, out of the booty, he gave twenty-five denarii each, twice that amount to each centurion, and thrice to each cavalryman.

The Roman historian Livy, in his History of Rome, *records M. Fulvius Nobilior's triumphs over the Aetolians and Cephallenia in 187 BC. A successful general always made sure his soldiers were rewarded for their efforts.*

The political rise of Rome was naturally reflected in the ever widening use of the denarius throughout the Mediterranean. Yet the Romans were nothing if not pragmatic and often allowed conquered kingdoms to continue minting their own coins, especially if they provided a reliable source of revenue. Thus both the kingdom of Pergamum, annexed in 133 BC, and the kingdom of Egypt, annexed by Octavian (later the emperor Augustus) in 30 BC, operated a semi-autonomous currency system, which enabled the Romans to extract a tax when people leaving these provinces wished to convert their currency to denarii. Equally the Romans were prepared to abolish a currency if it could be used to make a point. Following the Third Punic War (149–146 BC), Carthage was destroyed and Rome ordered its coinage to be removed from circulation and melted down.

Information about the use of the denarius in the provinces is relatively limited, although the New Testament of the Bible preserves some useful details about currency usage. For instance, Matthew 22:1–16 implies that a denarius a day was a fair wage for an unskilled labourer, although it seems unlikely that a labourer would receive this payment in one silver coin when his employer could pay in base metal coins. At 22:16–22 Matthew refers to the denarius as a 'coin of the tax', thus indicating the primacy of the silver coinage over base metal in the Roman revenue and taxation system. In fact the Gospels mention taxes for both the state and the Temple of Jerusalem which, for the latter's sacred purposes required payment in Tyrian shekels (see the chapter on the shekel). The money changers, vilified in the Gospels, nevertheless provided a vital service converting base metal coins into silver, or secular money into sacred. Although lucrative, the financial occupation carried high risks. According to the writer Suetonius (about AD 69–122), a money changer caught passing illegal tender could have his amputated hands nailed to his counting table, a punishment that even Suetonius thought to be a little extreme. By the time of Nero (emperor AD 54–68) most of the remaining local silver currencies had effectively become satellites of the mighty Roman denarius.

REVALUATION OF THE DENARIUS Around the time of the third and final Punic War (149–146 BC) the relative value of silver had increased compared with bronze. The denarius was revalued at sixteen asses, a change initially recognized with a mark of value XVI on the coin. This logically ought to have rendered the name 'denarius' redundant, since the word was derived from the ten to one exchange rate between bronze and silver. However, denarius was retained, suggesting that this Latin word now had a greater significance than merely the value of a particular coin. In time the XVI on the coins was also dropped, in favour of a barred monogrammed X, not dissimilar in spirit to the way in which an S is barred to form the $ symbol, or the L is barred to form the £ symbol. In addition to the denarius the sestertius, a quarter of a denarius, was revalued to four asses, but retained its name and symbol indicating its old value of two and a half asses, and the two became the main units of reckoning in written records.

Silver denarius of about 125 BC showing the cross-barred denarius symbol just below Roma's chin. The reverse features Jupiter riding a chariot drawn by elephants above the moneyer's name, C. Metellus. 3.89 g, 18 mm.

The success of the denarius was seriously tested in the first century BC. More money was needed than the available silver coins could supply to pay the military costs as the Roman Republic broke down in a series of civil wars. A gold denarius, 'aureus denarius', today called an aureus for short, was therefore introduced in about 80 BC. It was physically similar in size to the silver denarius, the obvious differences being the colour and its increased weight, because of the higher density of gold compared with silver. The aureus subsequently became a staple denomination under the Empire. Valued at twenty-five silver denarii, it was handy for the long distance traveller because he or she had to carry less. It is estimated that, if he survived to retirement age, a soldier could buy a farm with enough land to support his family for around sixteen of these magnificent coins, equivalent to 400 denarii.

Civil war also prompted a significant change in the appearance of the denarius, with portraits of living leaders appearing on the coins. Traditional Republican sentiment was typically averse to this, but Julius Caesar (100–44 BC) began to use coins to spread propaganda. He was the first Roman dictator to put his portrait on a denarius in early 44 BC, shortly before he was stabbed to death on the floor of the Senate. A year

This silver denarius was minted in Rome, shortly before Julius Caesar's murder on the Ides (15th) of March, 44 BC. Caesar is portrayed wearing a laurel wreath that conceals his baldness, together with the inscription 'Caesar, perpetual dictator', a title he had recently assumed. The reverse shows a complex arrangement of Roman symbols of power. Note especially the clasped hands on the left, a sign of trust between Caesar and his army, and the globe above, representing the Roman claim to world rule. 3.64 g, diam. 21 mm.

later, Marcus Brutus (85–42 BC), instrumental in Caesar's assassination, issued a bold riposte to this coin in the form of a denarius featuring his bust, two daggers and a cap of liberty. Caps of liberty were traditionally given to freed slaves. The inscription, 'EID MAR', refers to the Ides of March (15 March), the date when Julius Caesar was murdered. Ironically, while claiming to have restored the Republic, Brutus was also breaking with Republican convention by putting his own portrait on a coin.

Silver denarius commemorating the murder of Caesar, showing the head of Brutus on the front and a cap of liberty between two daggers on the back, 43–42 BC. 3.80 g, diam. 18 mm.

Denarii flowed into Rome, at first from plunder and later through taxation. The city became exceedingly wealthy and, while ancient writers complained that this was contributing to the moral decline of Rome's growing number of inhabitants, the writer Pliny (AD 23–79) noted that the flow of wealth was not simply one way. By the middle of the first century AD, he wrote, more than 25 million denarii were spent each year on luxury goods imported from China, India and Arabia. This figure is impossible to verify but the fact that denarii are often found in India suggests that there is at least some truth to the story.

PURCHASING POWER Often it is the case that wealth buys power and during the first century BC Roman Republican politicians spent colossal sums of denarii attempting to gain office. It was recorded, for instance, that Julius Caesar was 25 million denarii in debt shortly before he took office in 61 BC. He had to be bailed out by Marcus Crassus (about 115–53 BC), his plutocratic contemporary and later rival. Access to money provided political and military leverage and it is no coincidence that Octavian (Augustus), eventual victor in the civil war, was also the wealthiest individual in the Roman Empire, as were all successors to the office of emperor that he created.

The total sum which he [Augustus] donated to the public treasury, to the Roman plebs and to discharged soldiers was 600 million denarii.

Augustus' (63 BC–AD 14) inscriptional biography records his charitable endeavours, at the same time revealing his huge personal wealth.

The scale of the Roman monetary system had grown with the Empire and, by the second century AD the imperial budget is estimated to have been 225 million denarii per year, three-quarters of which was spent maintaining the army. Peacetime, or as the belligerent Romans probably saw it, preparing for war, was only slightly less expensive because Rome hung onto its vast empire by employing a standing army of some thirty thousand men. For most of the first century AD the annual pay of an average (non-promoted) soldier in a legion was 225 denarii. Soldiers were also paid a one-off recruitment bonus or 'viaticum' which was valued at three aurei, or seventy-five denarii, a third of their annual wage. It was intended to pay for a soldier's transit to his regiment at the frontier. This might seem like a large amount, but one should consider that a soldier might have to cross the whole of the Empire to reach his allotted garrison, a journey that could take months.

At the frontiers of the Roman Empire the denarius played a vital role in the economy of garrison towns. Letters written on wooden tablets found at Vindolanda near Hadrian's Wall in England provide a glimpse of the way in which the denarius was used as a unit of account. In a letter written in about AD 100 for example, Octavius, an entrepreneur supplying wholesale goods to the Roman army, wrote to his brother asking for money. References in the letter to deposits and cash advances sound strikingly similar to the modern world of financial transactions. One wonders if Octavius' request was successful, or if he lost his deposit on the grain he hoped to purchase.

Octavius to his brother Candidus: greetings...
I have several times written to you that I have
bought about 5,000 modii of grain, on account of
which I need cash. Unless you send me some cash, at
least 500 denarii, the result will be that I shall lose
what I have laid out as a deposit, about 300 denarii,
and I shall be embarrassed.

Extract from a letter found at Vindolanda on Hadrian's Wall,
about AD 100, now at the British Museum.

Production of the denarius intensified throughout the first two centuries of the Roman Empire, which may have contributed to a gradual lowering of its silver content from about AD 64 during the reign of Nero and the gradual debasement of the coinage accelerated in the third century AD. This reflected the accumulating military problems faced by the Empire, with expensive civil and foreign wars resulting in increasingly unstable reigns. Rapid turnover at the top was also a financial burden since emperors always had to effectively bribe their way to power. Already by AD 193 there had been an open auction between brazen political rivals to provide the biggest accession bonus to the soldiers. The apparent exhaustion of Spanish silver mines around this time, hitherto an important source of bullion, must have added to the problem. Inflation occurred which, together with the need for insecure emperors to incentivize military loyalty, compelled the state to drastically multiply the soldier's basic salary in just thirty years, from 300 denarii at the beginning of the reign of Septimius Severus (AD 193–211) to possibly as much as 1,800 under the reign of Maximinus I (AD 235–8).

The denarius was supplemented by a new coin, the radiate, probably at double its value but containing less than double metal content, hence another form of debasement of the circulating coinage. But this too became debased until it contained just a few per cent of silver. By the AD 260s there had been a complete breakdown in the link between the value of gold and silver coins. Indeed, the so-called 'silver' coins were virtually bronze by this point anyway. The consequence of this was that much of the actual bronze coinage was devalued to the point that it was worthless, causing a number of lower denominations to be scrapped.

The breakdown in the link between the value of gold and silver coins coincided with the climax of the Empire's third-century crisis: the breaking away of a number of provinces between about AD 260 and AD 274. The Empire was split in three and appeared to be on the brink of collapse until it was salvaged by the efforts of the emperors Aurelian (AD 270–5) and later Diocletian (AD 284–305) who divided its administration into more manageable parts. Aurelian attempted to reform the coinage by guaranteeing the silver content at five per cent, as indicated by the numbers appearing on the coinage, but more wide ranging reform had to wait until Diocletian.

Unusually, the impetus for reform of the coinage came not from Rome, but from the remotest part of the Roman world, from a ruler in opposition to the Empire. The British usurper Carausius (AD 286–93) produced a silver coin of a size and fineness that would have been recognizable to those who had encountered pre-debasement denarii. This innovative coin was first minted in Londinium (London) and was effectively adopted by the rest of the Roman Empire as part of Diocletian's coinage reforms in AD 294. It was possibly called a denarius but, confusingly, the old debased

Silver denarius of Carausius, minted in London, AD 286–93. Its reverse shows Oceanus, the divine personification of the seas surrounding Britain, rising out of the water with crab-claw horns and carrying a trident. 4.59 g, diam. 20 mm.

denarius was still a coin, albeit produced in small quantities.

To help people to understand where the new coin fitted within the currency (possibly after some form of adjustment to the system), inscriptions were reproduced all over the Empire in AD 301. Known as Diocletian's Currency Edicts, they were written in Greek and Latin, the two languages used for official purposes in the Roman Empire. The fine silver coin is listed as being worth 100 common denarii and was, by inference, probably called 'denarius argenteus', or silver denarius. Scholars tend to shorten it to just the hypothetical adjective, 'argenteus', to distinguish it from the 'classical' early denarius. The same year saw the issue of a separate Prices Edict, aimed at stabilizing the rising prices of the Empire but it failed to grasp the root of the problem, that of supply versus demand, and was doomed to failure. Nevertheless, the edict is useful for demonstrating that the 'classic' pre-debasement denarius continued to function as a unit of account. Sums of denarii were expressed in both the traditional currency symbol, the barred X, and the barred letter D. Prices were tariffed in 'd.c.', which stands for 'denarius communis' or 'common' (and, in other words, the debased) denarius.

Even the return of a fine silver coin could not solve the currency problems faced by the Roman Empire and further reforms were needed throughout the fourth century AD. During the fifth century AD, when the Roman West was crumbling, silver coinage was eclipsed by the use of gold. Nevertheless, the denarius did not disappear altogether. The Vandals, for example, a notoriously aggressive Germanic people who carved out a barbarian successor state in North Africa between AD 429 and AD 534, produced a series of silver coins denominated in denarii. Meanwhile, in the former Roman province of Gaul a Germanic tribe called the Franks established a kingdom, Frankia, forerunner of modern France. They introduced a new silver coinage in about AD 675; the early coins were stamped with the legend 'DENARIVS', later to become the French denier. The English penny was the equivalent of this coin which is why the letter 'd' continued to be used as shorthand for the penny's pre-decimal form up to 1971. In the eastern Empire after the transition from Roman to Byzantine rule the invading Arabs introduced a gold dinar, the name again derived from the denarius. In the 1960s the dinar replaced the Gulf rupee to become the official currency of Kuwait and Bahrain, and it remains the currency of several other countries.

Denarius also survives as, for example, 'dinero' in Spanish, 'dinheiro' in Portuguese and 'denaro' in Italian. Meaning simply 'money' the word reminds us of the once ubiquitous presence of the most widely circulated coin in the ancient world.

The Florin

I buon parenti, dica chi dir vuole,
a qui ne può aver, sono i fiorini

Cecco Angiolieri of Siena (about AD 1260–1312), after 1280.

'SAY WHAT YOU LIKE, florins are the best relatives', teased
the Tuscan poet Cecco Angiolieri in the later thirteenth century,
not long after the revolutionary new coin had been introduced to
its home city. This was Florence or Firenze ('Florentia' in Latin),
from which the coin derived its name; the 'fiorino' in Italian or
'florenus' in Latin and thus 'florin' in many of the languages of
medieval Europe. 'Quei son parenti, che nessum sen dole', they
are the relatives who will never give you grief. Cecco Angiolieri
lived in Siena, a close Tuscan neighbour to Florence. He might,
therefore, have been expected to be familiar with the golden
novelty represented by the florin. Yet its influence went far beyond
local notoriety, and few coins before the advent of a globalized
economy would come to have the impact of the florin. Its heyday
lasted for a century or so, but its legacy lasted much longer.

Introduced in 1252, the gold florin arrived after western
Europe had spent more than five hundred years with a monetary
world largely confined to silver. Economic historians have
suggested that the reasons why Europe withdrew from using gold
coins in the post-Roman world were a sheer lack of gold, a major
slowdown of commerce, changes in the nature of payments or
a complex mingling of these factors. The Florentine florin thus
became the main medium for the return of coins made from
gold, although it is worth noting that gold coins had never wholly
vanished from Europe. Some were imported from Byzantium
or the Islamic world and, on rare occasions there had been local
issues, but these were usually restricted and could never be called
regular currency.

By the mid-thirteenth century gold was available for coinage and gold coinage was, in itself, now useful and desirable. Primarily this was because it offered the Italian cities a compact means of storing and transferring larger sums, especially as regional and international trade increased. The cities of Italy, especially Florence, Genoa, Venice and Pisa, were increasingly dominating the economic life of the Mediterranean, pulling the trade routes in African gold from east to west. Already there had been a precedent for the florin in the shape of the augustale of Emperor Frederick II, king of Sicily (reigned 1197–1250, Holy Roman Emperor from 1220). Frederick II had access to the gold of Africa, especially West Africa, which crossed the Sahara to be put on boats at ports on the Mediterranean coast. The coin he introduced in 1231 was western-style in appearance but it followed the weight standards of Mediterranean coins.

The honour of introducing the first full series of gold coinage to medieval Europe has been disputed between historians of Florence and Genoa. It is now generally accepted that Genoa's genovino arrived slightly before the florin, but it was always a rather academic debate. There was never any question that it was the florin that quickly dominated the monetary scene, in Italy and then Europe as a whole, following its introduction in November 1252. The genovino did not receive the sustained scale and consistency of output necessary to give it the traction to compete as a currency.

Gold augustale of Frederick II of Sicily, 1231–51. He viewed himself as a successor to the Roman emperors of antiquity, which is why he is shown classically draped and wearing a crown of laurels. 5.20 g, diam. 20 mm.

Both coins were physically similar, being made from almost pure gold, having a diameter of 19 millimetres and weighing about three and a half grams. Each coin carried the symbols of its issuing city; the Florentine coin, for example, named and depicted its patron saint, John the Baptist. In this depiction he is wearing a belted robe with a rough goat-skin cape and a saint's halo surrounds his shaggy hair. His right hand is raised in blessing and in his left hand he holds a cross-headed sceptre. The other side presents a stylized lily flower with three petals and the Latin name of Florence, 'Florentia', literally meaning the blooming city. Both design and name were taken from the existing silver coinage but with the addition of 'd'oro', meaning 'of gold'. The design barely changed throughout the three centuries of the florin's existence, the only significant addition being a personal symbol placed after the saint's name on the reverse inscription. This indicates the civic official responsible for the issue of the coins, who typically held office for six months at a time.

Gold florin of the city of Florence, 1252–1303. 3.48 g, diam. 19 mm.

FLORENCE Built along the banks of the river Arno, Florence, or Firenze, has been the leading city of Tuscany since about AD 1000. Having prospered as a commercial centre from the fourteenth to sixteenth centuries, it was amongst the first cities to develop a sophisticated banking system. Florentine banking houses financed England during the Hundred Years War (1337–1453) and the Medici, in the fifteenth century the city's most influential family, were bankers to the papacy. Their patronage of the arts helped to turn Florence into the leading city of the Italian Renaissance.

The florin spread rapidly across Europe, carried by Florentine trade networks. It seems always to have been viewed as a trade coin and was probably never intended to be used solely within the city. International trust mattered more than internal convenience and the florin was of too high a value to function as a coin for daily use. It was worth a Florentine lira or 240 denarii (pennies) when first introduced, but this valuation was not automatically stable owing to the perennial challenge of operating gold and silver coins side by side. Nevertheless, the gold content of the florin was kept constant and the value of the coin was allowed to shift against the internal Florentine silver coinage. Thus by 1260, it had already increased in value from one lira, to one lira and five soldi. Almost everywhere in Europe reckoned money in the £sd system: a pound, livre or lira divided into twenty shillings, sols or soldi, divided into twelve pennies, deniers or denari. While this structure stayed the same almost everywhere, the coins were of different weight standards. Since, internationally, everyone knew how much gold was in a Florentine florin, it could be valued accordingly against local exchange rates.

Success usually encourages imitation and within a decade or so of the florin's appearance, Louis IX of France (reigned 1214–70) and Henry III of England (reigned 1216–72) had both issued their own gold coins. Neither coin explicitly conformed to the florin's standards but they were almost certainly inspired by its existence. The gold coinage of both countries was at first unsuccessful, but later kings of France and England did eventually manage to bring in long-lasting gold coinages. Coins of both kingdoms were initially based on a florin-derived weight standard but, in both cases they rapidly shifted to a standard that better fitted the local monetary system. In England, for instance, the Florentine florin was initially worth three shillings, a sum that was not exactly divisible into the pound, at twenty shillings. As a result the size (and hence the value) of its gold coins was established at six shillings and eight pence (eighty pennies), and three shillings and four pence (forty pennies). Both these denominations were divisible into the pound. The name remained familiar as 'florin' had, functionally, become the generic word for a gold coin. The word appears in Chaucer's *Pardoner's Tale* as a general term in which he conjures the image of a glittering and seductive gold treasure.

... floryns fyne of gold ycoyned rounde

Geoffrey Chaucer (about 1343–1400), Pardoner's Tale, *written late fourteenth century.*

The defining English medieval gold coin, the noble, began as 'the florin that is called the noble' and its French equivalent was the 'florin de l'écu'. These florins were minted to a different standard from the original florin and it was sometimes necessary to be specific about which coin was being discussed. In fourteenth-century English records, for example, mention is made of 'florins of Florence' or, even more descriptively, 'small florins of Florence'; since gold coins of the western kingdoms were usually physically larger.

Beyond England and France the model of the florin was much longer lasting. Many places simply made their own imitations, replicating the standards and design of the Florentine coin, but usually replacing 'Florentia' with the name of the local city or ruler. This happened in many of the principalities of the Rhone valley, the Netherlands and the Rhineland. There are, for example, florins from the cities of Bar, Orange and Vienne; Heidelberg, Koblenz and Bonn; Luxemburg, Flanders and Brabant. The city of Lübeck, at the margins of medieval Germany on the Baltic coast, produced a florin that was for a long time the only significant gold coin in northern Europe. Florins were also minted at Liegnitz in Silesia, in Austria and beyond into the kingdoms of Bohemia and Hungary.

The standards of the new coins remained, in theory, on a par with the original florin, even though the appearance might differ. Some issuers shifted to their own designs gradually, changing them at first on one side (replacing the Florentine lily with a local emblem, but retaining John the Baptist), and then on both, while others jumped straight to locally important symbols and images. The familiarity and trust built into the florin would, it was hoped, carry over into the new, local gold coinage. The German name gulden was effectively a synonym for the florin across most of these territories and gulden or guilders would, in England or France, be known as florins. In the fifteenth century English people knew the gold gulden of the states of the Rhenish Monetary Union as 'the florins of the Rhine'. The term 'florin' also survived in many areas as a separate accounting unit, based on a long-defunct valuation of the original florin.

Gold florin or gulden of Kuno von Falkenstein, archbishop of Trier, minted at Koblenz, Germany, 1362–88. The Florentine lily has been replaced by an armorial shield. 3.48 g, diam. 22 mm.

Throughout the fourteenth century the Florentine florin was used by the great Italian banking houses and by the huge financial network of the papacy, based in Avignon for most of the century. The coin was found almost everywhere in western and southern Europe and around the Mediterranean. In England King Edward III (reigned 1327–77) made grants of annuities from the port of London 'in florins of Florence', amounting to 1,000 in one instance. In 1338, Florentine merchants travelling between Romford and Brentwood in Essex were robbed by the locals of 160 of their florins.

Coin imitation could be a form of flattery, and yet poor reproductions could be a source of trouble. The Florentine government realized this and protested vigorously when local florins of less fine standards began, in their eyes, to pollute the currency pool of international trade and shake confidence in the original florin. The florins of the king of Aragon in Spain were a particular concern to Florence because they were a large and long-lasting issue of a relatively poor standard. There was also a new powerful Italian rival in the shape of the ducat or ducato of Venice, an easy alternative when trust in the florin faltered.

Engraving of a Florentine merchant by an unknown artist, about 1465. 179 x 100mm.

Gold florin of John I, King of Aragon, 1387–96. 3.34 g, diam. 18 mm.

A FLORIN FORGER GOES TO HELL We can get some
sense of the fervour with which the Florentines viewed the florin
in the pages of *The Divine Comedy* by the great Florentine poet
Dante Alighieri (about 1265–1321). One of the last damned spirits
he and we meet in the lowest pits of the Inferno is Master Adam, a
counterfeiter of florins. Master Adam was no ordinary back-street
forger: he was almost certainly supposed to represent Adam of
Brescia, employed by a rival Italian ruler to undermine the Florentine
coinage. In the real world he was, as he says, burnt at the stake in
1281. In Dante's Hell he sits in the Eighth Circle, the Malebolge or
'evil ditches', drowned and waterlogged among the forgers, liars
and leprous alchemists.

*O you, who are exempt from punishment in this grim
world (and why, I do not know), look and attend to the
misery of Master Adam. I had enough of what I wished,
when I was alive, and now, alas, I crave a drop of
water. The little streams that fall, from the green hills
of Casentino down to the Arno, making cool, moist
channels, are constantly in my mind, and not in vain,
since the image of them parches me, far more than the
disease that wears the flesh from my face.*

*The rigid justice, that examines me, takes its opportunity
from the place where I sinned, to give my sighs more
rapid flight. That is Romena, where I counterfeited the
coin of Florence, stamped with the Baptist's image: for
that, on earth, I left my body, burned. But if I could see
the wretched soul of Guido here, or Alessandro, or
Aghinolfo, their brother, I would not exchange that
sight for Branda's fountain....*

*Because of them I am with such a crew: they induced me
to stamp those florins that were adulterated, with three
carats alloy.*

From **The Divine Comedy** *by Dante Alighieri (about 1265–1321), written 1308–21.*

Venice had traditionally used the gold coinage of Byzantium to trade with and, so long as the coins remained of good quality, the preference persisted. By the 1280s, however, the terminal decline of the Byzantine gold coinage meant that this was no longer viable. So the Venetians introduced the ducat in 1284, a coin that deliberately replicated the standards of the florin. The ducat carried its own distinctive design featuring St Mark and the Doge (chief magistrate of Venice) on one side and Christ on the other.

tam bona et fina per aurum vel melior ut est florenus.

The order to introduce the ducat to Venice, on 30 October 1284, stated that it should be 'as good and fine gold as the florin, or even better.'

From around 1400 the ducat increasingly dominated Mediterranean trade, largely usurping the role of the florin. There were fewer direct imitations of the ducat to compromise its popularity and utility, although its standards were also widely copied, along with its name. 'Trade ducats' with local designs were eventually produced throughout early modern Europe by Dutch, German, Scandinavian, eastern European and other issuers. Even in Florence itself ducat became a word often used in place of florin.

The florin was also affected by broad trends in European coinage, particularly increasing supplies of silver. The early sixteenth century was a time of major shifts in the availability of precious metal. Silver was becoming increasingly dominant, with the revival of old mines and the discovery of new ones in Europe. From the 1540s, massive silver supplies arrived from Spanish America. Many of the florins and gulden of Europe changed from being small gold coins to large silver ones and the name followed the change. These were the only continuing reminder of the florin's days of medieval grandeur as even the silver florins themselves eventually shrank in size and purchasing power.

As the late medieval age of gold was fading before this new age of silver, the Florentine florin itself would soon cease to exist.

The last to be issued was produced in 1531, just as the Republic of Florence was being transformed into a hereditary duchy ruled by the Medici dynasty. It was replaced by a gold scudo, following the example of the Venetian Republic. This was a version of the French écu, less fine gold than the florin or ducat, but adopted in many Italian states in the early sixteenth century, responding to the impact of French armies and French money during the Italian Wars (1494–1559). In 1531 a financially desperate Republican government, having temporarily expelled the Medici, was searching for funds. It resolved to produce another coin to resolve its monetary crisis, as demonstrated in a report to the Florentine Council.

There being some quantity of gold in the mint that it would take a long time to refine, and wishing to help the city, which is in great need of great subventions and large amounts of money...and not wishing to violate in any way the goodness and purity of the ducato and Florentine gold, but rather to mint another coin not of the usual sort, in order to make some profit on it, following the example of another well-managed Italian republic, which, though in lesser difficulties than we, has used similar methods.

Report from the magistrates in charge of the mint to the Florentine Council, 1531.

Florence minted less fine French-style coins and used the Venetian term ducato for its own gold. Unlike Venice, however, it did not manage to restore the high standards of its gold coins. The Medici returned in 1533 but reviving the defining coin of the medieval republican tradition was not among their priorities. Instead coins proclaimed the power of the new dukes, with portraits and coats of arms. It was remarked that 'since all the old money of the city had the fleur-de-lis and St John on it, Duke Cosimo [de' Medici (ruled 1537–69)] destroyed and turned all the gold into scudi'. By now Florence had ceased to be the centre of a continent-spanning commercial and banking republic and was merely the capital of a territorial principality.

The legacy of the florin is perhaps most apparent in the long-continuing story of the Venetian ducat. Explicitly created as an equivalent coin, the ducat maintained its ancient standards until the end of the Venetian Republic in the nineteenth century. The ducat's empire had ranged well beyond that of the florin, deep into Asia and Africa in the early modern world, and Dutch trade ducats especially reinforced this global reach. The name also survived in many countries as a term for describing a mid-range silver coin, especially the Dutch gulden or guilder, which carried on into modern times as the large unit of the Dutch decimal system, divided into 100 cents.

The florin was even revived as part of a low-key move towards decimalization in Britain in 1849 when the British government decided to issue a two-shilling piece at a tenth of a pound in value. This fraction was a manifestation of the debate on the merits of a decimal system, already adopted throughout most of Europe and the Americas. One supporter of decimalization urged the introduction of this two-shilling piece as early as 1838, saying he would 'for perspicuity denominate the two-shilling piece, a Florin, as the name of the foreign coin nearest in value, and indeed a name not unknown in the English coinage'. Yet not everyone agreed, and some British newspapers stated that the 'designation will not be welcome to the public. It neither suits our language, nor brings with it any distinct association'. When it appeared the new florin, a highly attractive coin in a neo-Gothic style, proved even more controversial owing to the omission of 'Dei Gratia', 'by the Grace of God', and 'Fidei Defensor', 'Defender of the Faith'. The exclusion of traditional parts of British coinage inscriptions earned it the nickname of the 'Godless Florin'. Some commentators even linked the omission with a recent cholera outbreak, a form of 'divine retribution', it was supposed. However, it was not the only British coin to have omitted these inscriptions, and the whole saga has the modern feel of a bogus media storm.

Although full decimalization was a long time coming, the florin remained a part of the British currency system with the result that it entered the currencies of several countries within the British Empire and Commonwealth. This included Australia and New Zealand, and it was retained in the first coinage of independent Ireland. Ultimately, however, it was just an unremarkable part of a denominational series, and not the defining coin of the age. The modern florin survived until the belated introduction of decimalization in the UK in 1971, and in all related currencies at about the same time. The Dutch florin, or gulden, lasted longer, until the currency of the Netherlands disappeared with the introduction of the euro in 2002 and the last working florin was gone.

Silver 'Godless Florin' of Queen Victoria (reigned 1837–1901), 1849. 11.30 g, diam. 28mm.

The Franc

... coins of fine gold, to be called the francs of fine gold, which will be current at 20 sols tournois.

Ordinance of King Jean II le Bon, 5 December 1360.

THE NAME OF THE FRANC was chosen with a deliberate political purpose, and in this it stands apart from most other coins, whose names evolved more or less by accident. The name franc means 'free' and, while its etymology is linked to that of the name of France, the freedom in question was most probably that of a king of France, Jean II le Bon (John the Good), who ruled from 1350 to 1364. The occasion for proclaiming his freedom through a coin was his release from lengthy, if extremely comfortable, captivity in England. One of the great English successes of the Hundred Years War, begun in 1337, was the Battle of Poitiers in 1357 where the Black Prince, Edward III's eldest son, led his army to a victory that included the capture of the French king. A treaty settlement was agreed that included the fixing of an unfeasibly large ransom of 3 million livres. The livre, derived from the Latin 'libra', 'weight', was the equivalent of the pound. Once the agreement was made King Jean was allowed to return to France and he arrived in December 1360, announcing himself 'franc' (free) of the English, even though the ransom had yet to be raised.

Within days a new gold coin was introduced, apparently to celebrate his freedom and return, one now known as the franc à cheval, because the king was shown on horseback. An ordinance of 5 December, one of his first on his release, focused on the coinage and included the ordering of the franc. There is no question, therefore, that the name was official and used immediately. The coin was of course not simply a propaganda piece: in fact, medieval kings rarely used their coinage for propaganda. Instead it represented a new, strong currency as well as a repudiation of the monetary debasements and manipulations that had marked France in the previous few decades.

This interpretation of the origin of the franc is a strong probability, but it is not absolutely certain. No contemporary source states outright that the coin's name was a reference to the king's freedom and other explanations have been made, for example that the freedom represented is that of the subjects of France, who were to be free from all other taxes until the king's ransom was paid. Alternatively, it has been suggested that the name refers to France's mythic foundation by the Trojan exile, Francus. This echoes Aeneas's role in the foundation of Rome and is paralleled by a similar myth in Britain, this time with Brutus, another wandering Trojan founder.

It is certainly the case that the franc's design was unusual, because French kings were generally depicted on their gold coins peacefully enthroned, with sceptre in hand. Here instead the king was shown in armour and brandishing a sword, charging on his warhorse, implying that he is free and will resume the fight. In the event the only thing the king resumed was his lack of freedom. After about a million livres of the ransom had been paid, a vast sum in itself, the French decided that was enough and King Jean felt honour-bound to return to his admittedly enjoyable English captivity. He lived out his days with a sequence of banquets and tournaments, free from the burdens of government.

The gold franc continued to be issued as a coin into the reign of Charles V, Jean II's son. Within a year, in 1365, a new version was introduced, the franc à pied, which depicted the king standing in a gothic portico, though still mailed and holding a drawn sword as well as a sceptre. On Charles V's death in 1380, the franc

Gold franc of Jean II le Bon, 1350–64, showing the king charging into battle. Ironically, the coin commemorates a defeat. 3.77 g, diam. 28 mm.

ceased to be struck. The original franc à cheval type made a brief reappearance at a time of similar French troubles, when Charles VII succeeded to the throne in 1422. This was in the aftermath of the Battle of Agincourt and the Treaty of Troyes, which had brought much of France once more under the control of a king of England.

So, the original franc was a gold coin, one among many varieties of gold coins struck by French kings in the fourteenth and fifteenth centuries, and far from the most common or enduring. That was the écu, the principal French gold coin well into the early modern period. Why, therefore, did the franc name not fade into obscurity in the manner of other gold coin names of later medieval France, for example the chaise, the pavillon, the ange, the agnel and the royal?

The answer may lie in the value of the coin. Certainly the name was able to survive the disappearance of the coin and it did this by becoming an alternate term, or a nickname, for the French unit of account, the livre tournois, the most important of the several French pounds. The franc was valued at one livre tournois, or twenty sols tournois on its introduction, and officially retained that level throughout its existence. The other gold coins of the time and subsequent decades had different values: twenty-two and a half, twenty-five, twenty-seven and a half, thirty-three and thirty-six and a half sols tournois.

Yet, this does not wholly explain the persistence of the franc name. There was no need for an alternate name for the livre tournois, so it would appear that there are other reasons for its survival. Possibly the resonance of the word itself somehow created a positive reaction in the French monetary memory, along with its reputation as a piece of 'good' money. The similarity between franc and France may have also been a factor, although the complex relationship between these two words goes back much further and the connection has never found its way into any history book.

The franc remained in this ghostly state as an alternative name for the livre tournois until 1577 when it re-entered the physical world of the actual currency, though not for long. It was reintroduced under Henri III (king of France 1574–89) as part of a major reform. A gold écu of sixty sols tournois and a silver franc of twenty sols, or a livre, were the basis of the system in what had become a world dominated by silver-backed currencies. Indeed, production of this silver franc was deliberately designed to absorb the silver that was flooding into France from Spain's Flemish provinces. For ease of minting it was intentionally made of silver of the same standard as Philip II's daalders. In the event, this silver franc lasted

no longer than the gold franc before it and few were struck under Henri IV (reigned 1589–1610) and Louis XIII (reigned 1610–43). The half franc, which was struck more often, was revalued, so that the franc to livre tournois equivalence was technically terminated. In 1640–1 another reform jettisoned the franc as even a notional part of the system and for the rest of the Ancien Régime it did not appear in the physical currency, although there were, very occasionally, one livre coins produced. Instead the franc resumed its role as a nickname for the livre.

The franc might have disappeared from history after this but for the seismic political changes which took place after 1789 in the cataclysm of the French Revolution. Like so much else, the long-standing French monetary system was swept away. The currency underwent huge transformations and strains until a new settled system was introduced in 1795, Year Three of the Republic. Significantly it was a decimal system and, though not Europe's first (the Russian currency had been decimal since the early eighteenth century) it was probably the most influential, since it provided the model for the new dollar currency of the US. The name chosen for the main unit of the system, proclaimed in a decree of 15 August 1795, was the franc of 100 centimes. The new franc was equal to 101 livres five sols of the old system, reflecting the fact that the currency had been subject to major inflation during the early Revolutionary period. No explanation was provided in the proclamation for the choice of name.

Silver franc issued by Henri III of France, 1583. 13.87 g, diam. 35 mm.

Presumably, although the franc was a longstanding part of the French regal tradition, it combined this useful familiarity with a relatively informal previous status. Furthermore, it carried an association with both the concept of freedom or liberty and the name of France itself.

It took some time to stabilize the new monetary system as older money was purged from the currency, and part of this process included the commissioning of new designs for franc coins. Pictured is a design for a five-franc piece featuring Hercules standing between personifications of Liberty and Equality, designed by Augustin Dupré (1748–1843), chief engraver at the French Mint. His iconic design was unveiled in 1795 and was popularly revived in 1848, 1870–8 and on commemorative coins in the twentieth century. Containing 25 grams of silver, these high-value pieces, nicknamed 'hind wheels' due to their size, feature in Victor Hugo's masterpiece *Les Misérables* (published 1862). In one scene, set in the 1820s, a strange traveller in rags makes an unexpected purchase, deliberately overpaying for a pair of half-finished stockings that are being knitted by the orphan child Cosette, the novel's central character. Freed from the burdens of her work, she is allowed to run off and play.

The Choices of Hercules, design by Augustin Dupré, for a five franc coin, 1795.
185 x 173mm.

'I will buy that pair of stockings,' replied the man, 'and,'
he added, drawing a five-franc piece from his pocket, and
laying it on the table, 'I will pay for them.' Then he turned
to Cosette. 'Now I own your work; play, my child.'

[A bystander] was so much touched by the five-franc
piece, that he abandoned his glass and hastened up.
'But it's true!' he cried, examining it. 'A real hind
wheel! And not counterfeit!'

A bystander marvels at the generosity of a stranger in Les Misérables by Victor
Hugo (1802–85), published 1862.

Although accounting in francs became
compulsory in 1799 an actual franc coin was
not introduced until 1803, '7 germinal an xi'
of the revolutionary calendar. Germinal was
a month in the Revolutionary calendar which
ran from 21/22 March to 19/20 April. In the
same year, under Napoleon (1769–1821) as First
Consul, the Germinal Act was passed fixing the
ratio between silver and gold at 15.5 to 1.
A fixed ratio enabled the franc to be backed by
both gold and silver on a bimetallic standard.
At the same time the coinage was restored
with the silver franc, the franc germinal, at
its heart. There would be higher denomination
coins minted in gold, but the franc remained a
silver coin in the nineteenth century, and its design often featured
the current monarch or emperor of the various French regimes.
During the Second Republic (1848–52) a female head was
depicted, accompanied by the republican motto 'Liberté, Egalité,
Fraternité' (liberty, equality, brotherhood). At various times this
figure has been identified with Liberty, Ceres, the goddess of
agriculture, and Marianne, the personification of the Republic.
The same design was revived in 1871 by the Third Republic.

Silver franc issued by Napoleon as First Consul, 1803. 4.94 g, diam. 23 mm.

THE COUNT OF MONTE CRISTO In *The Count of Monte Cristo* (serialized 1844–5), Alexandre Dumas' (1802–70) classic tale of riches, revenge and redemption, francs pay for the eponymous hero's entrance to Parisian society in the 1830s. Once established the mysterious Count employs his enormous fortune to pay off the debts of his former allies but also to ruin the enemies who incarcerated him in a former life. In one memorable episode he turns up in disguise at the house of his beloved former employer and pays off his debts, valued at 287,000 francs, with 'a diamond as large as a hazel nut'. Meanwhile more conventional payment methods feature in the form of bonds and banknotes. Their appearance partly reflects the legacy of the French Revolution, during which the revolutionary government issued paper 'assignats', predominantly in livres, the unit of account that preceded the franc. These notes were intended to meet the financial demands of the new Republic but they were overprinted and became rapidly devalued. Nevertheless, their precedent established a template for the later printing of franc notes by the Banque de France, which was established in 1800 and was, from 1848, given monopoly over the issuing of banknotes in France.

In order to keep the franc on a bimetallic standard France had to maintain very high bullion stocks, far greater than any other nation. These large reserves permitted the relatively free flow of silver and gold bullion in and out of France. By buying whichever metal was depreciating in value and selling off the metal that was increasing in value, France was able to manipulate prices. Meanwhile, coinage production was adjusted according to whichever metal was least scarce. Before 1853 this meant that most of the coinage was silver. However, this switched to gold following the chance discovery of new gold deposits in the late 1840s. Between them, the mines of California and Australia at least doubled, if not tripled, the world's supply of gold. France responded by absorbing and processing up to forty per cent of all that was being mined, and in the years 1853 to 1866 huge numbers of five, ten, twenty, fifty and even one-hundred franc gold coins entered circulation, the latter weighing a substantial 32.25 grams.

France's ability to rely alternately or simultaneously on two metals has enabled it not only to use one or the other according to circumstance and offset the impact of their over-scarcity but also to come to the aid, not without profit to itself, of those of its neighbours which were lacking in either gold or silver. The Banque de France, as a vast reservoir of specie, has managed to satisfy the demands addressed to it from many sides.

Ernest Denormandie (1821–1902), governor of the Banque de France, 1881.

With the fixed silver to gold price ratio of 15.5 to 1 successfully defended, the bimetallic franc became an extremely stable currency in the early to mid-nineteenth century. It was perhaps confidence in its stability that inspired France, in 1865, to co-establish the Latin Monetary Union, an ambitious plan to unite the franc with the currencies of Switzerland, Italy and Belgium. The aims of the Union were to facilitate free trade by introducing a combined monetary system with coins of the same weight and fineness. Several other countries eventually joined and their currencies were aligned to make them freely interchangeable, with the French gold five francs being adopted as the base coin of the Union.

The Latin Monetary Union, like the franc, was initially based on a bimetallic system in which the relationship between the price of gold and silver was fixed. However, in the early 1870s the rapid rise in world gold production led several nations to back their currencies solely by gold. In the process of doing so they created an international gold standard. Three of them, the German mark, Japanese yen and US dollar, feature in this book. The UK pound, which also features, was already on the gold standard by the 1870s. Germany's switch to the gold standard was in fact facilitated by the defeat of France in the Franco-Prussian War of 1870–1. The indemnity imposed upon defeated France was set at 5 billion francs, a billion of which was to be paid equally in gold and silver coins. Germany, keen to increase its gold reserve, retained the gold but offloaded the silver. In most cases it was used to buy French exports, and it was said that many of the barrels of silver five-franc coins that crossed into Germany as part of the indemnity came back to France unopened.

Continued national rivalries and a gradual tendency towards gold destabilized the price of silver and, in 1873, it began to fall in price. In response the French government restricted the minting of silver to 280,000 francs a day, and finally suspended the production of silver coins in 1876. Minting in silver would eventually resume: indeed, one of the most iconic and oft-revived designs for a silver franc was first issued in 1898. However, despite this superficial continuity, the link between gold and silver was now severed, and the franc as a currency was now on a de facto gold standard.

Like most currencies, the franc was seriously affected by the international economic turmoil of the First World War. The Latin Monetary Union ceased to function during the war, well before its formal dissolution in 1927. Paper was substituted for gold in France, as in many countries, and convertibility was suspended, although the quantity of silver currency in circulation was initially increased to allay the concerns this aroused. Soon enough, however, all the French currency was paper or base metal and the coinage was, for several years up to 1931, produced by the French Chamber of Commerce, not by the government. Amid widespread inflation and a deficit crisis, in 1926 the new French prime minister, Raymond Poincaré (1860–1934), returned France to the gold standard, but at a level far below its pre-war parity. It was not until 1928 that parity was restored, with the franc, now an aluminium-bronze coin, equating to 65.5 milligrams of ninety per cent fine gold.

With the onset of the Great Depression, many countries withdrew their currencies from the gold standard to give themselves a wider range of strategies to aid economic recovery.

Silver franc designed by the sculptor and medallist Louis Oscar Roty (1846–1911), issued in France under the Third Republic, 1898. The coin shows Marianne, personification of the Republic, transformed into 'la semeuse' (the sower) and striding purposefully in front of a rising sun. A stylized version of the sower appears on modern French euro coins. 5.02 g, diam. 23 mm.

France initially chose a different path, accumulating gold reserves and seeking to preserve the value of the franc against gold through a deflationary economic programme. Although this served to enhance the international prestige of the franc, it became an overvalued currency. The strains of managing the different internal and external valuation of the franc eventually proved too much to sustain. In 1936 France finally left the gold standard and the franc was devalued.

In 1940 the French currency was disrupted by its defeat and partial occupation by Germany, and there were protests when the Germans fixed the franc against the mark at an unfavourable exchange rate. Between 1941 and 1944 currency was issued in unoccupied France, more usually known as 'Vichy France', as the État Français. Having negotiated peace with the Nazi regime of Germany, Vichy France adopted some of its extremist policies and a double-headed axe, a symbol of fascism, features on the franc coins issued during this period (see overleaf).

The purchasing power of the franc suffered a steady decline in the mid-twentieth century and three years into the Fifth Republic, in 1961, it had reached a point where it was an impractically small unit. The decision was taken to introduce a major wholesale

5000 franc note issued by the Banque de France, 1945. The franc suffered huge levels of inflation during the Second World War, resulting in much larger denominations of note. The female at its centre is an allegory of France, whilst the three men at either side represent its colonies. 210 x 113 mm.

revaluation, the first since it was inaugurated in 1795. The resulting new franc was equal to 100 old francs, but continuity was provided both by the survival of the franc name and by the revival of designs that harked back to the days of the Third Republic, with Oscar Roty's 1898 figure of France in front of a rising sun on the fifty centimes, one-, two- and five-franc pieces. For the ten francs the inspiration was even older, utilizing the 1795 design of the Choices of Hercules. Even silver was restored initially, with the five francs struck at the late nineteenth-century standard of eighty-three and a half per cent fine, and a ninety per cent fine standard used for the ten francs from 1965 until 1973. After 1974, however, there was no further precious-metal coinage issued for currency purposes and any of the older silver was demonetized in 1980. On the ten francs, an innovative new design was introduced to coincide with the shift from silver, featuring a stylized map of France.

From the start the new franc had a rival: alongside the pound and dollar, the German mark had established itself as a powerhouse world currency and, from the late 1960s, the international role of the franc wilted before the influence of the mark. This long process only ended with the introduction of the Economic and Monetary Union of 1999. The absorption of both mark and franc into the euro took with them two other European francs, those of Belgium and Luxemburg.

There is still a franc in Europe, however: the Swiss franc. Initially exported with the conquests of the French Revolution into the Helvetic Republic (1798–1803), the franc survived

Aluminium franc issued in Vichy France, 1943. It features a double-headed axe, symbol of fascism, and the name of Philippe Pétain, Head of State in Vichy France on its handle. The coin was made from aluminium owing to a wartime shortage of other metals. 1.30 g, diam. 22 mm.

Nickel-brass ten franc coin, 1975. 10.00 g, diam. 26 mm.

thereafter in several of the restored Swiss cantons and became the national Swiss currency in 1850. It became formally aligned with the French franc in the Latin Monetary Union and, having hardly changed its design in more than a hundred and fifty years, it has remained a safe-haven currency to the present day.

Across the world there are other francs, originating in the colonial French empire of the late nineteenth and twentieth centuries. Fourteen African countries use the franc CFA, a unit worth two francs in 1948, 0.02 new francs after 1960 and down to 0.01 francs in 1999, as the French franc transitioned to the euro. There are actually two CFA currencies, one for West and one for Central Africa, but they are effectively interchangeable. Although the currency emerged for use in former French colonies, a further country, Equatorial Guinea, a former Spanish colony, joined it in 1984. There is a similar franc, the franc CFP, in France's Pacific territories of French Polynesia.

For well over half of its six hundred and fifty year history, the franc has had a curious relationship with the French currency. At times it has been a nickname, at times a shadow and now it survives as the legacy currencies it has helped to spawn across the globe. Its persistence may well have a lot to do with its name, forever associated with freedom and independence.

From 1875 until 1951 the Banque de l'Indochine held exclusive rights to issue notes in the French colonies in South East Asia and Oceania. This 100 franc note was issued from 1939 until 1965 and features an image of a statue at Angkor in Cambodia, although it was actually overstamped for use in Papeete, the capital of Tahiti, in French Polynesia. 205 x 108 mm.

The Mark

The Germans are a great people deprived of certain attributes of sovereignty; with reduced diplomatic status. Germany compensates for this weakness with its economic power. The Deutsche mark is to some extent its nuclear force.

François Mitterrand (1916–96), President of France, 1988.

FRANÇOIS MITTERRAND'S comments may now have something of a period feel about them, but they give a sense of how the German mark of the second half of the twentieth century was, and indeed still is, viewed as a 'nuclear force'. Although the mark was the defining symbol of Germany's post-war recovery and modern economic might, such remarks forty years earlier would have raised nothing but incredulity. Fifteen years later the mark was just a memory, albeit a potent one.

The mark's story as a major and successful currency is historically very short, but there can be few major currencies with a prehistory as lengthy, since it began life as a weight standard before developing into a silver coin and unit of account. The Deutsche mark or D-mark of the Bundesrepublik and subsequently united Germany was merely the latest successor to a series of national German marks, all quite modern. Their tradition began with the proclamation of 1871 that created a uniform decimal currency for the brand new German Empire. To an adult living in about 1950, therefore, there might have been little about the mark's history that was worthy of mention. Indeed, its association with the hyperinflation of 1923 was probably what most people remembered about it. It seemed to lack the cachet of either venerable longevity or economic success. All this would change – and the mark's ancient roots help make sense of its revival and resurgence.

The earliest recorded references to the mark in any form come from ninth-century Anglo-Saxon England, the earliest probably in a charter of King Æthelwulf of Wessex of AD 857. The origin of the word itself may lie in Scandinavia and it is certainly Germanic, not derived from a Latin or Romance language. As a weight unit in use in Germanic northern Europe it was often specifically associated with weights of silver and gold. Indeed, until the twentieth century, measures of weight and money have sat together at a very fundamental level. The mark's story exemplifies this link more than most monetary units. Like the pound, it proved easy for the mark to do double duty by also serving as a measure of money, originating as the number of coins to be struck from a mark weight of fine silver.

By the central Middle Ages the mark had developed as a unit of account in parts of northern and western Europe. In medieval England, for example, the monetary mark was equal to two-thirds of the sterling pound: thirteen shillings and four pence, or a hundred and sixty pennies. There was never an English mark coin, although the high-value gold coins of medieval England, the noble and then the angel, were worth six shillings and eight pence, equivalent to half a mark or a third of a pound sterling. The English mark survived until about the sixteenth century, although it had a long afterlife: a lot of strange-looking rents and payments in early modern accounts look rather less odd when they are expressed as multiples or fractions of the old mark.

The earliest mark coins were introduced in Scandinavia and northern Germany at the beginning of the sixteenth century. New supplies of silver were sweeping across Europe and large silver coins were entering national currencies at the high end of the denomination range, often displacing small gold coins. The cities of Lübeck in 1505 and Lüneburg in 1506 were among the first to issue mark coins in Germany, and both cities had earlier struck fractions of the mark. For the most part, however, thalers and gulden remained the most important actual coins in use throughout Germany in the early modern period. In the north, the mark continued

Silver mark issued in Lüneburg, 1506, showing the town walls. 19.27 g, diam. 36 mm.

to serve as a monetary unit, without necessarily appearing as a coin. The independent imperial city and port of Hamburg was among the most important economic centres in Germany, a focus of money and exchange dealings and a true rival to Amsterdam and London. From the early seventeenth century the new Bank of Hamburg, founded in 1619, reckoned using a bank mark that never became a coin, but survived until the bank itself was closed in 1874.

THE MARK WEIGHT STANDARD As with all long-enduring and long-developing weight standards, there was no one 'mark', but a number of important and influential versions developed, which dominated regions and came to have international standing. Paris's Troy mark of about 245 grams of silver and London's Tower mark of about 233 grams were among these, while in the German lands there was the Viennese mark of 280 grams, the Nuremberg mark of 237 grams and the Cologne mark of about 234 grams. The use of the Cologne mark dates back at least as far as the eleventh century, and by the sixteenth century it was the most commonly used standard.

Germany during the medieval and early modern period was a vast assemblage of sovereignties and states that were part of the Holy Roman Empire. Indeed, not only was there no single mark weight standard and no single monetary mark, but also no unified German state. To provide a form of measure and, perhaps, to alleviate some of the confusion that was created by having more than one monetary mark, common standards were eventually agreed about the number of coins that could be struck from a mark weight. Sometimes this was part of the coin's inscription, as can be seen on a silver thaler of the city of Frankfurt am Main of 1772. Part of its inscription reads 'X ST EINE F M': ten struck from one fine mark.

Silver thaler of Frankfurt am Main, 1772, a 'tenth of a fine mark'. The coin features an accurate representation of the Frankfurt cityscape. 28.06 g, diam. 40 mm.

This was the history of the German mark before the late nineteenth century. It helped to embed the term within a number of states that coalesced in 1871 to form a new unified German state. The king of Prussia assumed the title of emperor of Germany and took direct rule of much of Germany. Along with the new state came a new national coinage, brought into being across a transition period of several years and assisted by the 5 billion francs reparations forced on France after the Franco-Prussian War of 1870–1. Unification also brought with it a centralized monetary policy and the creation of a central bank, the Reichsbank.

The new mark, decimally divided into 100 pfennigs, became legal tender across the whole German Empire in 1876. The choice of the mark as a name was said to be out of respect for the marks of Hamburg and Lübeck, owing to their ancient status and long stability. It may also reflect a decision not to make the potentially divisive choice between the thaler and gulden, traditionally used in north and south Germany respectively and which, although better known, were long established rivals. Like several late nineteenth-century currencies it followed the example of Britain and moved the German lands from a currency based on the silver standard to one based on the gold standard. There was a certain irony in choosing the mark for the main denomination of a currency based on the gold standard, given its long association with silver coins. The new one-mark coin did in fact remain silver, while higher value multiples were made from gold. The new coins featured the name and arms of the German Empire, with its single-headed eagle differentiating it from the double-headed eagle of the old Holy Roman Empire and current Austro-Hungarian Empire.

Silver mark issued in Germany, 1874. 5.52 g, diam. 24 mm.

The introduction of a national mark was part of a successful and simultaneous economic and political union, which helps to account for the staying power of the mark in the twentieth century, despite its many problems. Not only did the mark apparently originate as a genuinely German unit in the early middle ages, it represented the triumph of a united German nation, however partial and in some ways problematic the process had been. 'One nation, one currency' was a part of the formulation of national identity that coalesced in the nineteenth century. The process would be repeated across the world in the twentieth century as empires and countries disintegrated and were rebuilt, from the Turkish and Austrian empires to the Soviet Union. This in turn led to the emergence of new national currencies.

The new mark had many vicissitudes ahead of it and experienced high levels of inflation during the First World War, a trend that would have disastrous consequences in 1923. As with the other powers, Germany expected a short war and, having refused to raise taxes, instead sold war bonds through the Reichsbank to fund the war effort. Patriotism and the promise of good returns just about financed the first two years of the war, but increasingly the banking system had to be relied upon. The convertibility of money into gold was suspended and vast amounts of token paper money were issued.

The end of the war brought new pressures to the German economy and inflation continued unabated. Between the armistice of November 1918 and the signing of the Treaty of Versailles in July 1919, for example, prices rose by about fifty per cent. Under the terms of the Treaty, Germany's geography was redrawn, resulting in the loss of several coal and iron-ore producing regions and a corresponding reduction in German exports. The actual sum of reparations was not agreed in the Treaty but by the Reparations Commission which, on 1 May 1921, specified the amount at 132 billion gold marks. This was shortly followed by the so-called 'London ultimatum' in which the terms of these repayments were set, and Germany was given six days to accept, the penalty for non-compliance being occupation of the heavily industrialized Ruhr region. The payments were huge: around a third of all government expenditure in the years 1921 and 1922. But through the effects of inflation and by taking on short-term debt, the government was initially able to cope. There was even, albeit briefly, optimism on foreign markets that the mark would recover its former value, leading overseas investors to buy security bonds. But then political instabilities, social unrest and domestic demand for higher wages began to have an impact and Germany defaulted on its reparation payments in January 1923. In response, Belgian and French troops marched into the Ruhr. Unable to respond militarily, the Weimar government instructed workers to engage in passive resistance. It brought factories and mines to a standstill, and yet to avoid even more civil unrest, the government had to guarantee that it would maintain wages. The only way it could achieve this was by printing more notes.

At this point, high inflation became hyperinflation and, with Germany on the brink of civil war, the mark went into meltdown. At the height of the crisis, the Reichsbank had thirty factories producing paper and twenty-nine producing printing plates. Even this did not meet demand for production, and a further hundred and thirty-two printing firms were employed to meet the deficit. Millions of banknotes were printed every single day, with the result that the value of marks in circulation increased from 120 billion in 1921 to an astonishing 497 million trillion in 1923. The political

500 million mark banknote issued by the German Reichsbank, 1923. 155 x 85 mm.

fallout from the crisis weakened the government, causing the German chancellorship to change hands twice between August and November 1923.

EMERGENCY MONEY A by-product of the inflation of 1914–23 was the issuing of 'notgeld', or 'emergency money', by various municipal authorities throughout Germany. Denominated in both marks and pfennigs, these helped to alleviate demand for Reichsbank coins and notes, and their status as currency was recognized by law in 1922. Notgeld was mostly printed on paper, but some authorities utilized locally available materials and industries to produce them. The notgeld of Bielefeld in north-east Germany, for example, were made from linen, while those of Meissen in east Germany were made from porcelain. Thousands of different designs and variants were issued, and printed notgeld often feature scenes from German folk tales or from the region in which they were issued. Owing to the variety of colourful designs, they became very popular with collectors.

Paper notgeld issued for use in Hamelin, Lower Saxony. The design of the note features a scene from the German folk tale 'The Pied Piper of Hamelin', the story about a rat-catcher, or 'rattenfänger', hired by the town to rid it of its rodent population. 100 x 65 mm.

The hyperinflation of the mark caused chaos for ordinary Germans. Stories abound about how people had to fill whole wheelbarrows with banknotes merely to go out and buy a loaf of bread. Counting the notes out would have been too time consuming, so shopkeepers instead resorted to weighing bundles on scales to determine their approximate value. Those lucky few with access to 'hard' currencies such as the dollar found that their money now went a long way, but those whose income was solely in marks were less fortunate. Salaries were adjusted according to price increases, but the inevitable time lag between adjustment and actual payment meant that workers were often paid less than they should have been, given the rate of inflation. Unsurprisingly, perhaps, a black-market economy developed and people from the cities travelled to the countryside, desperate to barter their personal items for basic produce. Among the biggest losers were those on fixed incomes and those with savings. William Guttmann, who co-authored a book about the inflation, wrote about his own father's experience as a wealthy retired businessman living in Germany at the time.

A Berlin woman starts her stove by burning banknotes. During hyperinflation of the mark in 1923, it became cheaper to burn notes than fuel.

He was, by middle-class standards, a rich man and
intended to live as a rentier *on the proceeds of his*
investments. These were mainly life-insurance policies,
fixed-value securities, among them a lot of war loans,
and the biggest single item was a mortgage on a large
agricultural estate of 300,000 marks, whose yield of 15,000
marks per annum would have provided a very good income.
All this depreciated, of course, to zero – my father managed
to keep his head above water by resuming some work.

The Great Inflation: Germany 1919–23 *by* W. Guttmann *and* P. Meeham, 1975.

Sweeping reforms were required to end the madness. In
October 1923 a stable interim currency, the 'rentenmark', was
created, its value based on mortgaged property. Then, in 1924,
the old mark was put out of its misery and replaced by a new
gold-backed mark, a reichsmark, which was worth a trillion old
marks and pegged to the dollar. All other circulating currencies
were withdrawn at the same time. The decision to back the
reichsmark with gold was intended to restore its international
credibility. At the same time war reparations were renegotiated
in Germany's favour. The German economy during the Weimar
period would remain weak, but the currency was now relatively
stable and would remain so until the onset of global depression
in 1930–1.

The experience of 1923 had a deep and unsettling impact
upon Germany's monetary policy. It led subsequent governments
to oppose inflation, even when the collapse of the international
gold standard and overvaluation of the mark in the early 1930s
made it desirable. Ideological resistance to a mark revaluation
persisted under the Nazi dictatorship of Adolf Hitler (1889–1945).
He often blamed inflation for having brought about the end of the
German Empire, and any devaluation would have compromised
his rhetoric. Yet the Third Reich's commitment to rearmament
had a devastating impact on the economy, and a successful
devaluation of the French franc in 1936 made a corresponding
devaluation of the mark seem, to some observers, like an attractive

proposition. By 1938 Josef Goebbels, minister for propaganda, believed that Germany was on the brink of collapse, and noted as much in his private diary.

The financial situation of the Reich is catastrophic.
We must look for new ways. It cannot go on like this.
Otherwise we will be faced with inflation.

Josef Goebbels (1897–1945), December 1938.

In January 1939 the Reichsbank directorate wrote to Adolf Hitler to warn him that inflation of the reichsmark was now impossible to avoid. The response from Germany's chancellor was characteristic: 'this is mutiny!' he exclaimed, and promptly sacked Hjalmar Schacht (1877–1970), president of the Reichsbank. In the event the Third Reich's ministry of economics reasoned that Germany was heading almost inevitably toward war and that the resolution of its monetary problems could probably stand to be delayed. Not for the first time, Germany's leaders entered a war gambling on the assumption that the loser would pick up the tab. Indeed, it became clear even from the outset of the war that insufficient controls were in place to prevent inflation, and the government abandoned any pretence at trying. Unrestricted money creation resulted in depreciation of the reichsmark, which in turn led to a growing black market. By the end of the Second World War barter and the use of unofficial currency, nicknamed 'cigarette currency', was widespread.

The end of the war saw Germany occupied and divided into zones, the westernmost of which were controlled by Britain, France and the US, with the eastern zone controlled by Soviet Russia. In the western zones the impetus for currency reform came from the US which, in 1946, began to devise a secret plan to replace the unstable and greatly devalued reichsmark with a new currency. The plan noted that 'monetary reform constitutes an important step towards the ultimate goal of allied economic policy in Germany; the development of a peaceful, democratic, reasonably decentralized economy'. Economic rehabilitation was seen as essential, and the launch of the Deutsche mark, or D-mark, in the western zones preceded even the creation of the new German Federal Republic.

In June 1948 the US Army distributed a new currency in the Western occupation zones of Germany. These banknotes, which had been printed in the United States, carried no signatures and made no mention of an issuing authority. But they did carry the name Deutsche Mark. Seldom has a military initiative created such a successful brand name.

Albrecht Ritschl, economist, 2001.

The introduction of the D-mark took the Soviet regime by surprise: all zones had, in theory, been working towards unilateral reform of the German currency. In practice diplomatic relations were already tense and an agreement between the eastern and western zones was never likely to be workable. Nevertheless, Soviet occupation authorities were highly critical of the western powers for having abandoned the reichsmark, and publicly announced that 'it completes the division of Germany'. Plans were now hastily drawn up for currency reform in the Soviet zone, leading to the creation of the ostmark. Like the other Soviet bloc currencies, the ostmark of the new East German state, the DDR, had minimal international exchange value. Competing ideologies and the onset of the Cold War would ensure that the marks of East and West Germany would take very different paths over the next forty years.

The new West German currency, like the new state of the Federal Republic of Germany, was based from the very beginning on ideas of European integration and revival. The D-mark was both instrument and symbol of Germany's recovery, and Germany set itself resolutely against the recurrent instability that had dogged the mark ever since German unification in 1871. For the architects of economic reform, for example Ludwig Erhard (1897–1977), the chubby-faced, cigar-smoking German economics minister from

1948 until 1963, safeguarding the D-mark was a top priority. It helped West Germany's economy to recover at a rate faster than any other European nation in the 1950s and, by 1960, it accounted for one-fifth of all world trade in manufactured goods.

Nevertheless, there would be troubles to be overcome and the mark's chaotic historic legacy remained an inhibiting factor. For example, a revaluation of the mark in 1961 as a result of difficult economic conditions caused enormous soul searching, while another revaluation in 1969 dominated the German general election and contributed to a change in the ruling coalition. Just as inhibiting was the government's reluctance to increase circulation of the D-mark.

Hyperinflation of the old mark had left a legacy of fear within Germany's central bank, the Bundesbank, that if the D-mark were allowed to become a reserve currency to rival the dollar, it might devalue.

This led the Bundesbank to adopt a cautious approach with regard to the D-mark's growing international status as currency. Indeed, in the late 1970s it went as far as to discourage some central banks from acquiring D-mark reserves. In the 1980s monetary policy was relaxed, and it was the international strength of the D-mark that, in 1988, led the French president François Mitterrand to define it as Germany's 'nuclear force'.

The greatest challenge to face the mark was the reunification of Germany in 1989 and the currency union that followed in July 1990. At the time of reunification the East German economy was on the verge of collapse. Inevitably, the East German mark had to be converted at a level above its real value to avoid a devastating

The new copper-nickel D-mark coin was introduced in 1950. Its design, showing the German eagle on one side and oak leaves on the other, remained unchanged until Germany switched to using the euro. This example was issued in 1994, the last year in which mark coins were minted for circulation. 5.53 g, diam. 23 mm.

impact on the East German population, but there was conflict over the level agreed and the result was inflationary for the overall German economy.

The D-mark was symbolic of German economic success, yet it was in some senses transitory. Post-war European leaders were committed to economic and political integration, culminating in the creation of the European Economic Community (EEC) or Common Market in 1957. Plans for an Economic and Monetary Union (EMU) began formally in 1970, but the suspension of dollar to gold convertibility in 1971 and an oil crisis in 1972 caused plans to be abandoned. Discussions were only formally resumed at the Hannover Summit held in 1988, attended by governors of the national banks of the twelve member states of the EEC. When the EEC was absorbed into the newly created European Union in November 1993, it listed the establishment of a single currency as one of its objectives.

The mark finally met its end at the turn of the millennium with the creation of the Eurozone in 1999 and the issue of the euro in 2002. German leaders looked back to the early days of the first mark to justify the monetary union, as later noted by Helmut Schmidt, German Chancellor from 1974 until 1982.

We had a currency union up to 1914 in Western Europe – the Gold Standard. From a historical point of view, I would draw a direct parallel.

Helmut Schmidt (1918–), 2007.

There are few, if any precedents, for the winding up of a highly successful currency and its replacement by a new one. The disappearance of the mark in 2003, along with several other major European currencies was, therefore, an extraordinary development. Surrendering the D-mark was neither easy nor welcome to many Germans and their leaders and there were very deep misgivings in the public and media. It had become a talisman of success and prosperity to West Germans and a symbol of hope for the future to East Germany.

Termination of the D-mark was in some ways a move of political expedience. European monetary union was one way for Helmut Kohl (1930–), German Chancellor 1982–98, to assuage widespread international concern about the extraordinarily swift process of reunification. It was a placatory gesture that signified a mightier Germany surrendering its metaphorical 'nuclear weapon'. The unification of 1871 had brought the modern mark into existence, yet the reunification of East and West Germany had provided the catalyst for its end. Such a step had always been a likely consequence of policy trends in the late twentieth century, with a political momentum that proved hard to resist. For Germany, more than for other member states of the European Monetary Union, the euro provided a continuation of the same monetary policies that had contributed to the success of the mark. Thus the new European Central Bank was, at German insistence, based in Frankfurt, with considerable continuity from the German Bundesbank.

The mark that began as a weight standard in early medieval Europe ended as a modern monetary unit, imbued with its value by the state's guarantee and the trust that its users, inside its own country and internationally, placed in that guarantee. Its modern history demonstrated painfully the fragility of that trust. As a national currency, it was born out of the nineteenth-century nationalist movement and it ended in an economically globalized world. The history of a currency is part of a complex mixture of trust and belief and the history of the German mark provides a curious example of retention after failure, and surrender after success.

The Rupee

*The Rupiya is round, and it weighs eleven
and one half mashas. It was first introduced
in the time of Sher Khan.*

Āini Akbari (Life of Akbar), about AD 1590–6.

INTRODUCED AS A COIN in the mid-sixteenth century AD,
the rupee came to prominence under the Mughal Empire before
becoming the standard coin of British India in the nineteenth
century. Its use spread primarily as a result of Indian Ocean trade,
and today a number of countries in south Asia have national
currencies denominated in rupees or a rupee-derived equivalent.

Medieval India had little need for a unified coinage, which
only arrived with the establishment of the Mughal Empire in
the sixteenth century. Before this the country was divided among
hundreds of competing kingdoms, large and small, with a wide
variety of languages, religions and customs. As the *Life of Akbar*
suggests, the rupee was most probably introduced by Sher Shah
Suri or Sher Khan, 'Lord of the Tigers', as he was popularly
known. Sher Khan was not a Mughal emperor; he was in fact
born in Afghanistan in 1486 but went on to found many of the
administrative structures later adopted by the Mughals. His
father was a high ranking official who served the Lodi dynasty,
which ruled much of northern India. Following in his father's
footsteps, Sher Khan commanded part of the army of the Lodi
dynasty that tried to recover control of Delhi in 1526 from Babur
(1483–1530), the first Mughal emperor. Through a cunning display
of strategy, Sher Khan managed to simultaneously betray the
Lodi leaders to their deaths and successfully repel an attack by
Babur's son, Humayun (1508–56). Humayun withdrew to deal
with insurrection in another region. For the next ten years Sher
Khan extended his power base from the state of Bihar in north-

east India, primarily at the expense of neighbouring Bengal until, in 1536, he was ready to re-launch his campaign against the Mughals. Having lured Humayun's army into Bihar he trapped and destroyed it at the Battle of Chausa in 1539, although Humayun was able to escape into exile. Sher Khan, meanwhile, was now undisputed ruler of almost all northern India.

Having consolidated his rule, Sher Khan began a series of reforms to maximize revenue from his subjects, including the introduction of the rupee, a new silver coin weighing between about 11 and 11.6 grams. The *Life of Akbar* states that the rupee was 'perfected in [Sher Khan's] reign and received a new stamp'. It primarily replaced the shahrukhi, a thin coin weighing a little less than 5 grams, and the tanka, a heavy east Indian coin similar to the rupee. Sher Khan died in 1545 when he was blown up in an accident involving military explosives. The fragile political unity he had worked hard to establish gradually disintegrated until his successor lost control of Delhi to Humayun, who returned from exile in 1555.

Silver rupee coin issued by Sher Shah Suri (Sher Khan), minted in Sharafibad, modern Pakistan, 1540. 11.01 g, diam. 25 mm.

Rather than dismantle Sher Khan's reforms, Humayun and then his son and successor Akbar (reigned 1556–1605) chose to retain the rupee and it became the key silver coin in a monetary system that also featured gold and copper coins. Under Aurungzeb (reigned 1658–1707) Mughal authority spread throughout all but the southernmost tip of India, and the use of the rupee extended to include the disparate communities under Mughal rule.

ANCIENT ORIGINS The word rupee is derived from the Sanskrit root 'rūp' which means to 'stamp' or to 'form'. It is generally accepted that the term was in use for centuries prior to the 1500s as a generic word for coins, which may explain why it was so readily adopted as a name for a specific coin. The rupee was often known by other names, for example 'akbari' or 'jahangiri', named after the ruler who issued the coin, but these terms rarely outlasted their reign. As well as the rupee the Mughal Empire had copper coins, called 'dam' and gold coins called 'mohur'.

Although the rupee became the standard silver coin under the Mughal Empire, initially it played no role in overseas trade. This was because the first commercially successful European voyages to India, in the early seventeenth century, mainly carried Spanish pesos, the key trade coins of their day. The first English voyage, which set sail in 1601, was financed by the Company of Merchants of London Trading with the East Indies, later to become the East India Company. In its infancy the Company periodically sent fleets to India and, in 1608, it began to use Surat to dock its ships, establishing its Indian headquarters there in 1615. Other trading ports followed at Bombay, Calcutta and Madras. Spanish pesos provided a practical means to pay for Indian goods but the Company realized that it needed to simplify trade by sourcing coins that were compatible with Indian weight standards. By 1643, the Company was minting small gold pagodas which circulated successfully in south India but were less widely accepted in areas of Mughal control further north.

The Company finally decided that it needed to mint its own rupees but this proved problematic because Mughal rulers were unwilling to grant licences for their production. The Company attempted to strike its own coinage bearing European designs in

1672 but soon found that only coins with Indian designs would be readily accepted beyond its sphere of influence. Between 1685 and 1690 it tried to force the issue by waging an unsuccessful war, commonly known as Child's War, with the Mughal Empire. After paying a hefty indemnity to the Mughal emperor Aurangzeb in 1690 a licence was finally secured permitting the Company to mint rupees in the name of William III and Mary (reigned 1689–1702) inscribed in Persian. Aurangzeb nevertheless forced these to be discontinued in 1695 because they cited 'the name of their impure king'. From then on the Company was obliged to issue rupees in the name of the Mughal emperor. It continued to produce silver rupees with the name of the emperor until 1835, long after the Company had, in fact, usurped Mughal authority. The collapse of Mughal rule in the mid-eighteenth century transformed the East India Company from armed merchant enterprise to colonial overlord, ruling large parts of India both directly and indirectly.

As the Company took over the production of coinage it opened more mints and began to introduce minting machinery imported from England and, in the process, it gained access to the vast and lucrative system of taxation that had previously underpinned the authority of the Indian princely rulers. There appears to have been a great deal of opportunity for corruption. An anti-Company pamphlet published in 1773, for example, describes how Indians were interrogated to reveal where they hid their rupees. Torture had supposedly enabled Company officials to amass rupees in 'lacks and crowes'. The author meant lakhs (100,000) and crores (10 million), the south Asian units of reckoning. Although the pamphlet was sensationalist it did highlight the fact that the collection of taxes was often haphazard and unfair. In the Sherpa district near the border with Bangladesh, for instance, overzealous zamindars (tax collectors) working on behalf of the Company in 1820 were alleged to have collected 20,000 rupees from a region that had been assessed at only 12,000 rupees.

The silver rupee held a relatively high value and in the mid-1700s one coin could purchase about fifteen kilos of rice. Company agents were paid well in comparison with their Indian subjects. In the early 1800s, for example, a junior employee of the East India Company earned about a hundred rupees per month and would be expected to spend about half his salary on an extensive household of servants. This included a khidmutgar (butler) salaried at eight rupees, a dhobi (clothes washer) and cook at six each, a punkah wallah (fan operator) at four and a sweeper at three. Sixteen rupees provided for the wages of the syce (groom) and for horse fodder.

A rupee coin was supposedly worth its weight in silver or, at least, very close to that value: the mint needed to retain a small amount to cover its running costs. As a coin became worn from circulation silver would be lost, reducing the weight of the coin. The loss in a coin's bullion value was acknowledged during the reign of Akbar when the most recent coins to enter circulation, known as 'sicca', were valued higher than older coins. Older coins could still be redeemed, at a discounted rate, when presented at the mint. However, the sicca system was open to abuse since the treasury would often accept new coins but would insist in only paying out in old rupees. This ensured that the treasury always profited by the exchange. European travellers to India found it equally vexing and in 1676 the French traveller Jean Baptiste Tavernier (1605–89) published an account of his visits to the Mughal court. Suggesting that the problem was widespread, Tavernier noted that 'the poor people who do not know how to read the year when they coined these rupees or paisa are subject to be cheated'.

The problem with sicca persisted under the coinage of the East India Company. Money changers would often devalue Company rupees, forcing it to mint new coins, even if there were enough coins already in circulation. The Company attempted to put a stop to this by minting coins with a fixed date, and coins bearing the name of Shah Alam II (reigned

Silver rupee issued by the East India Company under the name of Shah Alam II, dated to the nineteenth year of his reign (1778), but actually minted in 1819. 12.39 g, diam. 26 mm.

1759–1806), dating from the nineteenth year of his reign, were minted for nearly thirty years after his death. The practice achieved only limited success owing to the continued circulation of rupees that followed local traditions. In 1835 the Company resolved to create a standard machine-made rupee for the whole of British India, featuring the bust of King William IV (reigned 1830–7). A mint was built at Calcutta to supply the new uniform rupee and the system of sicca was thus abolished. To discourage its revival, rupees bearing the year 1835 were struck continuously until 1840, and it was only then that they were replaced by coins of Victoria, even though she had been on the throne since 1837.

Rupee banknotes were slow to develop, even though the idea of transferring money through written documents such as bills of exchange or cheques was well known in India before the arrival

Silver rupee issued by the East India Company featuring the head of William IV, dated 1835. 11.63 g, diam. 30 mm.

250 sicca rupees note issued by the Bank of Hindostan, 1820s. Although the bank is thought to have issued notes from the 1770s, no earlier specimens are known to have survived. Circulation of these notes was limited to Calcutta. 190 x 116 mm.

of Europeans. Known as 'hundi', these were traded primarily between merchants. The first rupee banknotes were printed for the Bank of Hindostan in 1770 but the refusal of the East India Company to recognize them for the payment of taxes and other dues limited their usefulness. In 1859 a Scottish economist named James Wilson (1805–60), who had recently arrived in India, proposed to establish a national issue of rupee notes. He died only a few months later but his vision was achieved in 1861 when the Bank of England was awarded the contract to print a new series. However, these first notes were easily forged and had to be withdrawn almost immediately. A more complex design was needed, which was introduced in 1868. It was not until 1928 that the Indian government opened its own note-printing facility at Nasik, a major railway junction in central India. The paper for the notes was supplied by Portals, an English company that also supplied the Bank of England.

DIRECT RULE In 1857 there were large scale revolts against the East India Company which were only suppressed after a bloody conflict. The British government reacted by assuming direct control of the Company and thus it took full responsibility for the administration of India, including its currency and taxation. From 1862 coinage was issued under the name of Victoria as sovereign ruler of India.

If it were not for the rupees I would not stay in the confounded country for an hour.

The words of an anonymous British soldier, reported in The Times. The opportunity to loot and plunder proved to be a major incentive to the soldiers sent to crush the Indian Mutiny in 1857–8.

Use of the rupee spread to other countries as a result of trade and commerce, as well as as an extension of colonial rule. The formal annexation of India made it by far the biggest British dominion in Asia, boosting a process that had already begun under the East India Company. The rupee circulated in the Gulf States following the imposition of a General Treaty in 1820, Sri Lanka in 1836, the annexed parts of Burma in 1857 and Mauritius in 1872. From 1902 the Chinese government minted imitations at Sichuan. In East Africa, including Kenya, Uganda and the Rift valley, the rupee circulated unofficially for decades until it was officially adopted as the main unit of account in 1905. Conversely, domestic use of the rupee in India itself remained limited. As late as the 1950s, for example, it was estimated that nearly half of all rural transactions took place through a barter system without coins or notes.

India's rupee was backed by silver rather than gold and the currency received a major shock when the price of silver began to fall after about 1873, leading to a devaluation of the rupee against gold-backed currencies that included the pound. It hampered India's ability to pay for imports and to pay Britain for its administrative costs, known as 'home charges'. The question of how to respond to the falling value of silver vexed politicians and economists and, in 1892, the British government of India formed the Herschell Committee to address the problem.

Cecily, you will read your Political Economy in my absence. The chapter on the Fall of the Rupee you may omit. It is somewhat too sensational. Even these metallic problems have their melodramatic side.

The Importance of Being Earnest *by Oscar Wilde (1854–1900),* *first performed 1895.*

In 1893, based upon the committee's recommendations, the Indian government fixed the exchange rate between the rupee and the pound so that one rupee was equal to one shilling and four pence. This partially separated the value of the rupee from its relative value in silver and, since sterling was based on a gold standard, the rupee was now also effectively backed by gold.

THE 'PIG' RUPEE In 1911 a rupee was issued showing the bust of George V (reigned 1910–35) appearing to wear a pig on a chain around his neck. The design, by the Australian sculptor Sir Bertram Mackennal (1863–1931) had been poorly engraved, and was in fact supposed to show an elephant. The engraving was re-done the following year to limit the offence that could be caused to religious communities in India.

Silver rupee of George V, 1911. 11.69 g, diam. 30 mm.

The engraver attempted to reproduce the details of a heraldic collar – that of the Order of the Indian Empire – which the King is wearing, and has succeeded in making the little elephants which hang from it look exactly like pigs.

Yorkshire Evening Post, *February 1912.*

During the First World War the British government of India increased taxes from one and a half to two and a half rupees per head, to help pay for the costs of the conflict. This contributed to the impoverishment of communities, especially in rural areas such as the village of Pimpla Sondagar, near Poona. In a survey conducted there in 1916 the ryots (peasants) of the village, numbering 556 (of whom a quarter were children), had a combined annual income of 22,500 rupees but, between them, the villagers were 13,300 in debt, upon which they paid 2,600 rupees in interest payments. Tax avoidance later became a tool for Indian resistance to British rule, particularly when Mahatma Gandhi (1869–1948), leader of the Indian nationalist movement, masterminded a mass defiance of the salt tax in 1930. The Indian author Munshi Premchand wrote a novel called *Godaan* in 1936 which focused upon debt cycles in an Indian community. The protagonist's daughters are named after the Hindi words for gold and silver and the author puns upon their names whilst highlighting the importance of silver to the Indian economy.

...gold is just for admiring from afar, it is silver that is actually used. If it weren't for Rupa [silver], how would money be minted?

Godaan *by Munshi Premchand (1880–1936), 1936.*

Towards the end of the First World War the global price of silver began to rise and the rupee was revalued upwards against the pound to two shillings and four pence. A strong rupee enabled the Indian government to clear its budget deficit but, from the British perspective, reduced the purchasing power of the pound against the rupee. This was particularly problematic in the British-ruled East Africa Protectorate, where European settler farmers accrued debts in rupees but had an income that was often in sterling. In late 1919 the British government responded by establishing the East African Currency Board, which forcibly demonetized the Indian rupee in British East Africa. There was an ideological element to the Board's actions: it signalled a reassertion of British colonial rule in the region and a deliberate severing of its economic ties with India. As a replacement the Board experimented in issuing its own version of a rupee, then a florin, before finally settling upon issuing a shilling currency, at a par with the British shilling, in 1921. Elsewhere too, the influence of the Indian rupee was becoming diminished: Afghanistan abandoned the rupee in favour of the afghani in 1925, and Burma would revert to the use of the kyat in 1943 after the end of its occupation by Japan.

Throughout the 1920s the Indian rupee remained pegged to sterling and, with no central bank to guide monetary policy, the stability of the rupee was dependent on factors that were largely beyond India's control. The Wall Street Crash in 1929 and subsequent Depression led to a fall in commodity prices which caused a contraction in India's money supply. It put the rupee under enormous pressure to devalue but Britain refused permission, on the grounds that modifying the rupee-sterling exchange rate would make it more expensive for the Indian government to service its sterling debt. Instead India resorted to exporting gold to meet its external obligations, which increased in price after the pound (and, by association, the rupee) left the gold standard in 1931.

The Depression would have far reaching consequences for Indian monetary policy. In the first instance, in a bid for greater stability, it led to the creation of the Reserve Bank of India in 1935. Initially it was a private bank licenced to print government currency notes, the first of which appeared in 1937. The Reserve Bank would fund India's participation in the Second World War by overprinting notes, and the ensuing inflation served to exacerbate a famine in Bengal in 1943. Furthermore, the Depression brought the relationship between the rupee and sterling into question, with Britain accused of manipulating rupee exchange rates to prop up the value of sterling. The reality was somewhat more complicated, but it served to support the Indian nationalist argument that British colonialism was inherently self-serving, and was a major contributory factor enabling India to gain independence in 1947.

The dismantling of colonial empires that took place at the end of the Second World War provided newly independent countries with the opportunity to create new national currencies. For those that had previously used a rupee currency, such as India, Pakistan and Sri Lanka, continuity was maintained and their new national currencies were also denominated in rupees. For Indonesia, in the grip of a revolution between 1945 and 1947, adoption of the rupee-derived rupiah was part of a wider military and diplomatic struggle between the Dutch colonial government and the native Republican government. The region had been under Japanese military administration since 1942 and, for monetary expedience, Japanese military currency continued to circulate on Java and Sumatra after the Japanese surrender in 1945. The Dutch were keen to re-establish a version of the pre-war Netherlands Indies guilder. But the Republic wanted to issue its own rupiah currency, not least because it realized that a new national rupiah carried propaganda value as a symbol of independence. The British

Foreign Office attempted to mediate and, concerned that a Republic-issued rupiah could increase political divisions between the two sides and undermine economic stability, it opposed its introduction. Ignoring British and Dutch resistance, the Republic went ahead and issued its first rupiah notes in 1946. However, it would not be internationally recognized as a currency until the end of Dutch colonial rule in 1949.

In India, the first independent rupee notes were issued in 1950, prominently depicting a pillar of Ashoka where there had previously been a portrait of the British monarch. In 1987 the Government of India reintroduced portraiture on the notes, this time featuring an image of Mahatma Gandhi,

Twenty-five rupee note issued by the Government of Indonesia, 1947. The note features a portrait of Sukarno (1901–70), leader of the struggle against Dutch colonial rule and first President of independent Indonesia in 1949. 168 x 79 mm.

500 rupee note issued by the Reserve Bank of India, 1987. 167 x 73mm.

in recognition of his efforts to secure a peaceful transition towards independence.

In the years that followed independence, India withdrew from trade and investment with Western nations, maintaining the rupee at an artificially high exchange rate to discourage imports. The rupee continued to be used by the Gulf States, yet the wider circulation of the rupee posed a risk for the Indian government. In the event of a run on its reserves, it could not afford to exchange their equivalent value in sterling. Specific Gulf rupees were issued for use in the region in 1959, but in 1961 Kuwait announced that it would begin a phased replacement of the rupee with the Kuwaiti dinar. Negotiations with Kuwait about its withdrawal from the rupee dragged on until, by the mid-1960s, India was afflicted by war with Pakistan, crop failure, famine, an adverse trade balance and the suspension of foreign aid upon which it relied. These same pressures forced the government of India to devalue the rupee from 4.76 to 7.5 to the dollar in 1966, without first consulting the countries that used it. It wiped more than forty-two per cent off the value of the circulating notes, a devaluation that was greeted with uproar by the Gulf States and further pushed them towards establishing independent currencies. By 1970 none was still using the rupee.

In self-imposed isolation from the West, and at the height of the Cold War, India turned to the Soviet Union, coming to rely upon Soviet aid and oil. Soviet oil was purchased through barter, by exporting goods such as tea, rather than with exchangeable currencies, a practice that became known as 'rupee trade'. Rupee trade lasted until the Soviet Union began to experience economic difficulties in the late 1970s. Its decline and eventual collapse coincided with an easing of exchange rates and India's rupee was allowed to devalue to more realistic levels. But the lack of a free floating exchange rate made it difficult for India to maintain its balance of payments, and it experienced a deficit from 1985 to 1990. Having exhausted its foreign currency reserves and heading toward a default, the government was forced to devalue the rupee in 1991. By the late twentieth century India's rupee was pegged to a basket of currencies of its major trading partners but high inflation persisted, and in 2007 the rupee appreciated twelve per cent against the dollar.

Conversely, problems endured by the rupee were met by increased support from the Indian government, which pledged to promote its strength as an international currency. In March 2009 the government announced a competition to create a symbol for the rupee, which had previously been depicted by the letters 'Rs' or a barred letter 'R'. The winning design by Udaya Kumar was announced in 2010 and the new symbol resembles both the English 'R' and the Nagari character for 'ru' also intersected with a bar, ₹.

I think our Rupee suffers from not having an identifiable symbol. With a symbol we would be poised to represent our economic liberalization as, perhaps, quite soon the Indian currency will be traded globally.

Nondiat Correa-Mehrotra, finalist in the competition to design a symbol for the rupee, 2010.

Today the rupee remains the currency of almost a quarter of the world's population. It is used in India, Indonesia (as the rupiah), Maldives (as the rufiyaa), Mauritius, Nepal, Pakistan, Sri Lanka and the Seychelles, and has survived the rise and fall of both the Mughal and British Empires. Almost five hundred years after its introduction, it offers one of the best examples of continuity despite immense political, economic and social change.

The Yen

It is the intention of the Government to adopt a system of coinage which shall be in consonance with the best usages of the nations of the world, and to issue new coins in accordance with this system.

The New Coinage Act of Japan, *1871*.

FOLLOWING THE END of two and a half centuries of a policy of national seclusion, in 1871 Japan completely overhauled its monetary system and introduced the yen. From its inception, the yen was to play a major part in Japanese attempts to re-engage with the wider world.

Since the late 1630s Japan had been largely closed to foreigners. Entry was forbidden under penalty of death. It was ruled by the Tokugawa shogunate, a military government based in the city of Edo (modern Tokyo; hence the period is sometimes known as 'Edo'). Then, in 1853 and again in 1854, a squadron of navy ships arrived from the US to demand trading rights. The sudden opening of Japan to foreign trade caused enormous economic, political and cultural upheaval, resulting in high unemployment and bankruptcies. Foreign investors found to their delight that Japan's gold coinage was undervalued by about a third, compared with its global price. Its gold coins were exported in huge numbers and quickly disappeared from circulation. Paper money was issued instead, but without the backing of gold its printing caused inflation. In 1867 Tokugawa Yoshinobu (1837–1913) abdicated amid near civil war and the Meiji government (Meiji meaning 'enlightened rule') took over. It was keenly aware of the strength of the western nations. To bring Japan onto an equal footing it pursued a policy called 'fukoku kyōhei', meaning 'rich country, strong army'. Embassies were dispatched around the world to ascertain the best ways for Japan to modernize, paving the way for currency reform and the introduction of the yen.

The new coins were first announced in March 1868 and almost every aspect of their size, design, weight and even their shape represented a conscious break with tradition. Because of their shape, chosen to emulate European-style coins, the new coins were named 'yen', meaning 'round' (the yuan and won currencies of China and Korea mean the same thing). Previous shapes of metal money had included the large gold oval ōban and kōban, the silver rectangular bu and shu, long bar chōgin and bean-shaped mameita-gin. In fact the only older Japanese coins to which the new ones bore a resemblance were cast round copper alloy coins with a square hole in the middle, known as 'sen'. The sen was subsequently designated at a hundredth of a yen, and a third unit, the rin, became a thousandth, but was dropped in 1892. The previous accounting units of ryō, bu and shu, which had been named after weight terms, were all abandoned.

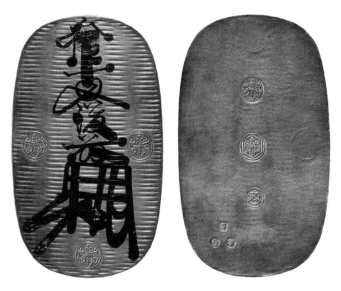

This gold ten ounce (ryō) ōban issued by Tokugawa Iemochi in 1860 was one of several types of coin to circulate in pre-Meiji Japan. 113.13 g, 134 x 81 mm.

The mid-nineteenth-century trading standard in east Asia
was the silver dollar, but vice-minister of finance Itō
Hirobumi (1841–1909), who had studied the monetary
systems of Britain and the US, recommended putting the
yen on the gold standard 'in accordance', he said, 'with the
best teachings of modern times'. A compromise was reached
in which Japanese silver dollars were created for use in foreign
trade and gold for domestic use. In gold the yen weighed
1.5 grams, while its silver coins, at 26.95 grams, were just
under Mexican dollar weight. Being underweight discouraged
their circulation beyond Japan's trade ports. In effect, Japan
was simultaneously trying to put the yen on two standards.

Gold proof ten yen coin, minted at Osaka, Japan, 1870 (issued 1871).
16.40 g, diam. 32 mm.

THE IMPERIAL MINT

It is in Osaka that the new Japanese mint is established, and the people are very proud of their beautiful gold and silver coinage, which steam power and ingenious mechanism send forth with teeming rapidity.

British travel agent Thomas Cook (1808–92) is impressed during his visit to the Imperial Mint during his round-the-world tour in 1872.

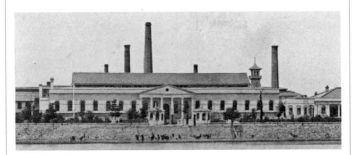

The Japanese Imperial Mint at Osaka from *The Sphere*, 1905.

Until the Meiji restoration Japan's coins were made from copper alloy cast in moulds following the Chinese tradition and silver and gold pieces cast and hammered following the tradition of making ingots. However, to fulfil its aim to match the yen with the 'best usages of the nations of the world' the government decided that the new coins should be machine struck using the latest technologies. It resolved to build a new mint at Osaka and commissioned a red-brick building from the British architect Thomas Waters (1842–98). The machinery was purchased in Hong Kong where, conveniently enough, a state-of-the-art mint happened to be for sale. It had been built by the British in the 1860s hoping to supply silver coins to China, but the enterprise had proved unsuccessful. The government wasted no time in acquiring the mint and shipped it to Osaka, along with its master, the British technician Thomas Kinder (1817–84), and a number of overseas experts. Despite a fire which destroyed some of the equipment, the mint was quickly up and running, producing its first coins for circulation in 1871. Kinder's contract and that of almost all the foreign overseers was terminated in 1875 after a petition of officials convinced the government that the mint could be run more efficiently without them. It was also claimed that the decision was partly made because Kinder had been arrogant and rude toward employees.

There was, however, just one problem: Japan lacked the necessary gold reserves to keep the yen on a gold standard. Furthermore, the fall in the global price of silver in the 1870s created an imbalance within the currency. Foreign traders began to buy up and export gold yen coins using overvalued silver yen. Silver dollars, although supposedly restricted to port districts, increasingly had to be used in domestic trade owing to the absence of gold coins, and were legally permitted to circulate within Japan in 1878. The foreign press was scornful about the failure of the gold standard and its damaging effect on Japan's international status. One newspaper serving a Japanese port community remarked derisively that 'she wished to place herself on some imaginary footing with England and America'.

Pre-Meiji Japan was already familiar with paper money and in the 1860s foreign banks based in Yokohama issued western-style notes. From the beginning the yen was also issued as a paper currency but to start with the notes had deliberately ignored western styles. They were taller than they were wide, copying 'hansatsu' (domain notes) and other monies from the Tokugawa period. But in 1872 problems relating to quality, security and counterfeiting prompted the government to commission its notes from a printer in Frankfurt. In the same year the National Bank Act was passed following the example of the American national bank system. It allowed privately funded national banks to issue western-style notes, which were at first printed by the Continental Bank Note Company in New York until production moved to Japan in 1877. The banks were named numerically and 153 had been established by 1879. The wealth of the banks was considerable and in 1877 the government borrowed from the Fifteenth National Bank in Tokyo to meet the military expenses of the so-called Satsuma Rebellion, a revolt of disaffected samurai.

However, the paper currency began to have an inflationary effect on the yen. In response the government stopped issuing new licences and in 1880 helped to found the Yokohama Specie Bank, instructing it to purchase silver bullion and coins. By issuing paper silver certificates in their place the Yokohama

Yen note issued by the First National Bank in Tokyo, 1873. The note was engraved by the Continental Bank Note Company in New York. It shares a number of characteristics in layout and colour with the US dollar bill, the greenback, issued ten years previously. 190 x 81 mm.

Specie Bank helped to concentrate Japan's silver into a central reserve. Japan adopted a policy of increasing exports, extending loans to exporters in paper yen and then taking payment in coins received from goods sold abroad. As a result the Yokohama Specie Bank quickly became important for dealing with foreign exchange, setting up office in the Japanese consulate in London in 1881.

In the meantime a plan was put forward to formalize the yen as a currency by establishing a government-backed central bank to regulate the national and specie banks. The Bank of Japan (Nippon Ginkō) was established in 1882 and issued its first note in 1885. It features the god of wealth, Daikoku, holding a mallet and bales of rice, an image that would have been familiar to many, having previously featured on silver

mameita-gin. The Bank of Japan helped to reduce domestic prices and restored the paper currency at a par with silver. Its notes were the first to be fully convertible to silver. Meanwhile national banks were now prohibited from issuing new notes and were gradually reorganized into deposit banks. Many retained their numeric names and the First National Bank, the Dai Ichi Ginkō, went on to become one of the world's largest private banks. Circulation of government and other banknotes was prohibited from December 1899 and so, by 1900, the yen consisted solely of coins and banknotes issued by the Bank of Japan.

The 1890s were a crucial period for the development of the yen and policymakers were keen to extend its circulation throughout Asia, similar to the way in which sterling freely circulated around the British Empire. To bring this about, in 1895 the Japanese government annexed Taiwan as part of the settlement that ended the 1894–5 Sino-Japanese War. Japan established the Bank of Taiwan, a yen-issuing central bank, in 1899. The war had been fought with China primarily over a controlling influence in Korea, as Japan attempted to broaden its political and economic influence in South East Asia. Similar

Yen note issued by the Bank of Japan, 1885. The note features Daikoku, one of the seven gods of fortune. He holds a golden mallet and sits on a bale of rice whilst mice (symbolizing plentiful food) scurry around below. 134 x 78mm.

attempts would bring Japan into conflict with Russia ten years later. For the next four decades the yen would take centre stage in a policy of Japanese overseas expansion, through which the so-called 'yen bloc' was formed.

The Sino-Japanese War had other far-reaching benefits for the yen, which was still based on a silver standard. The price of silver was volatile and its fall in price caused the yen to decline against currencies that were on the gold standard, making it more expensive to import goods. An opportunity to move back to a gold standard presented itself during peace negotiations with China, when an indemnity of 230 million silver taels (356 million yen) was exacted, a huge amount that equated to about a quarter of Japan's annual income. It paid off Japan's trade deficits, curbed inflation, and the remainder was deposited in the Bank of England, which now agreed to reverse a previous decision and open an account in the name of the Yokohama Specie Bank. The amount was converted to gold and then shipped to the Bank of Japan. There was a lot to be moved, the largest amount ever drawn on the Bank of England, and the Japanese government accepted the payments over several years. The value of the yen was reset to gold at 0.75 grams. This was half its previous value, reflecting the fact that the gold to silver price ratio had also halved since 1871. Gold coins worth 74 million yen were minted in Osaka, but did not enter circulation, and instead the Bank of Japan issued notes backed by gold from its new reserve.

With the yen now on the gold standard, it could be used to borrow on London's financial markets. In 1898 the Bank of Japan was yet to have a London office, so instead the Yokohama Specie Bank dispatched its vice-president, Takahashi Korekiyo

Gold twenty yen coin minted at Osaka, 1897. Ten yen and five yen gold coins were also minted when Japan joined the gold standard, as well as six smaller denominations in silver, copper-nickel and bronze. 16.65 g, diam. 28.5 mm.

(1854–1936), on a delicate mission to negotiate a loan of 200 million yen (100 million US dollars). This proved difficult because Japan was still largely an unknown entity on the international markets. Its gold standard was new and its record in defending it was hardly unblemished. Despite valiant efforts, Takahashi secured merely 10 million yen. By 1904 he had moved to the Bank of Japan and he was dispatched once more to raise a loan. Japan needed funds to wage war with Russia over Korea. This time the outcome was successful and Japan was able to borrow approximately 800 million yen (300 million US dollars or 82 million pounds sterling). These loans were on paper only and, as Wakatsuki Reijirō (1866–1949; prime minister of Japan 1926–7) later explained, 'even though England lent gold to Japan, not one ounce of gold went from England to Japan'.

Korea had been forced to open to Japanese trade in 1876 and Japan's first overseas bank set up there in 1878, although the yen was not introduced until 1902 when the Dai-Ichi Bank was granted permission to issue notes. Yi Yong-ik (1854–1907), the Korean emperor's financial advisor, resisted its imposition, instead favouring Korea's traditional Chinese-influenced alloy coins. However, his arrest in February 1904 removed a major obstacle to its expansion and by the end of the year, 3.37 million yen in Dai-Ichi banknotes were circulating. In 1905 the Korean mint was closed and the gold standard was implemented. Dai-Ichi notes were, in theory, fully convertible to gold, but in practice most were only redeemable for securities and bonds. It could be said that Korea's yen currency was backed by a note reserve in Tokyo that was, in turn, backed by gold held in London.

At the same time, Japanese interests were also extending to Manchuria (north-east China) and the Yokohama Specie Bank opened its first branch there in January 1900, before issuing silver-backed dollar notes in 1903. In this way the Specie Bank became a forerunner for semi-imperial control of Manchuria, just as the Dai-Ichi Bank had in Korea. In Manchuria it was deemed too risky to immediately introduce a gold-backed yen, since it was feared that it might encourage speculative trade between China's silver-backed currency and the gold-standard yen. Instead the Specie Bank was instructed to unify the yen currency on a silver standard. In 1913 the government gave the Yokohama Specie bank permission to issue yen notes in Manchuria backed by gold coins or Bank of Japan notes, but Japanese coins and notes did not themselves circulate.

Foreign loans had fuelled the building of the yen bloc, but they increased Japan's susceptibility to international monetary crises. By 1914 the national debt stood at a quarter of Japan's annual income and the outbreak of war in Europe put a stop to foreign loans. Additionally, the suspension of gold exports froze all gold reserves held abroad and Japan briefly entered a recession. For a while the US was the sole supplier of gold to Japan until in 1917 it too implemented a gold embargo, forcing the yen off the gold standard. However, the overall result of war in Europe was more positive for Japan and for the yen. Its export market boomed and Japan became a creditor nation for the first time. In 1915 the Banque Franco-Japonaise (Nichi-Futsu Ginkō) arranged the first yen loan to France and in 1916 the Yokohama Specie Bank raised loans to Russia and Britain. These loans enabled other countries to buy Japanese consumer goods, leading to a rapid increase in the standard of living and a boom in the luxury goods market. The war period was later criticized as a time of unnecessary excess and decadence.

If the war represented a time of excess, the 1920s were characterized as a period of economic stagnation with the yen remaining off the gold standard. The US had reinstated its gold standard shortly after the war, and gold once again flowed into Japan. However, Japan hesitated to put the yen back on the gold standard and with convertibility suspended, inflation ensued. Gold convertibility came close to being restored in 1923 but the plan was disrupted by sheer bad luck – the death of the prime minister Katō Tomasaburō in office in August, and a large earthquake that struck the Tokyo-Yokohama area in September, destroying both cities and causing some 140,000 deaths. The Bank of Japan's gold vaults came close to being destroyed in the resulting firestorm. Another attempt to restore the gold standard was made in 1925, but speculative buying of yen pushed its value too far out of alignment with gold. As the decade wore on, the Japanese government had another reason to stockpile gold: it was preparing to expand into Chinese territory, for which substantial reserves would be required.

China is disordered and chaotic, but sooner or later, a time of national stabilization must come. Then, in order to govern the country and pacify the people, the first thing you will need is gold, for laying railroads, establishing industry and so on...In that case, Japan must definitely be ready to lend at once as much as 500 or 600 million yen in gold.

Takahashi Korekiyo (1854–1936), speaking as finance minister in 1928.

Despite the recession, the 1920s also witnessed the transformation of Tokyo as a centre of international finance. The Bank of Japan presided over the introduction of trade bills and bankers' acceptances as a means of financing trade. It insisted, albeit unsuccessfully, that trade bills should be denominated in yen for payments in China and other Asian countries. A gold-standard yen on a par with the major international currencies remained desirable and it was finally reinstated in January 1930. However, amid global economic crisis and the collapse of the international gold standard, the timing could not have been worse. Within a year, 250 million yen in gold had left Japan and the Bank of Japan had to decrease banknote issue accordingly. Fewer yen in circulation caused prices to deflate, directly affecting suppliers who had stocks of goods. Japan's biggest export at the time was silk, and the entire industry went into recession. In December 1931, less than two years after it had been reinstated, the gold standard had to be abandoned. Bank of Japan notes continued to carry the phrase 'convertible to gold' until 1942, but the phrase was now meaningless.

The failure of the gold standard and the 1931 invasion of Manchuria by the Japanese caused the value of the yen to plummet against world currencies. In 1936 the Japanese author Nakano Shigeharu (1902–79) commented on its falling value in his poem 'The Rate of Exchange'.

If one yen is not two marks
And it happens that it's not half a mark
If on the whole the yen is not a mark and not
a pound or a ruble or any of these things
What is this darn thing called one yen?

From 'The Rate of Exchange' by Nakano Shigeharu, 1936.

Like several other currencies in the 1930s, the end of the gold standard and subsequent fall in the yen's value prompted a dramatic change to how it looked. Coins no longer held intrinsic value and in 1938 the first aluminium coin was introduced, valued at one sen. After the outbreak of the Pacific War in 1941 the Printing Bureau of the Ministry of Finance could not print enough notes, so production was outsourced. Watermarks were simplified and serial numbers were removed, while the shortage of metal for coins meant that notes worth less than a yen were now issued. In 1945 the government introduced a 1,000-yen note and even considered issuing ceramic coins.

Japan's surrender in September 1945 signalled the end of its empire and the dismantling of the yen bloc. Under allied post-war occupation, continued note shortages were met by the issuance of so-called military yen, but to avoid further disruption to the currency the Japanese government recalled them in autumn 1946. In Okinawa, however, under occupation until 1972, the US military government issued various forms of military scrip.

In 1948 the US banker Joseph Dodge was brought in as financial advisor to the occupying allied forces; he implemented a policy of self-sufficiency through foreign trade, the so-called 'Dodge line', which helped to bring inflation under control and fixed the yen at 360 to the dollar. Japan's post-war diligence at maintaining the exchange rate helped to bring about phenomenal economic growth. Japan's 'economic miracle', as it came to be known, curbed inflation and yet unlike the Greek drachma and German mark, no yen revaluation was attempted. As a result, Bank of Japan notes were now issued in denominations of up to 10,000 yen while in 1953 the almost valueless sen was abandoned. A small aluminium one-yen coin featuring a sprouting branch was introduced in 1955 and the same design continues to circulate today.

The 360 yen to the dollar exchange rate deliberately undervalued the yen to ensure that Japanese exports remained competitively priced. When America abandoned the gold standard in 1971, a move that would lead to floating exchange rates, the yen immediately soared to around 300 to the dollar, revealing the extent of the undervaluation. From the early 1970s until the mid-1990s Japan's economic growth ensured that the value of the yen continued to rise. It also nearly doubled in value against the dollar in 1985 following the signing of the Plaza Accord, an agreement between five industrial countries to depreciate the value of the dollar in relation to the yen and Deutsche mark. By April 1995 the yen had peaked at less than 80 to the dollar and Japan's economy almost matched that of the US. As a result of low interest rates on borrowing and the generous spending of Japanese tourists, circulation of the yen overseas also increased significantly. The value of notes repatriated to Japan via foreign banks had stood at 1.6 billion yen in 1980, but reached 10 billion by the mid-1990s. At the time forecasters predicted that the yen might challenge the dollar and the mark for the prestigious mantle of the world's most widely circulated currency.

The continued expansion of Japan's economy and its international trade may yet lead to an expanded role for the yen as a key currency, though not for some time.

Takatoshi Itō (1950–), economist, 1994

Aluminium yen coin minted at Osaka, 1994. The design and composition of the yen coin has remained unchanged since 1955. 1.00 g, diam. 20 mm.

Then, in the late 1990s the bubble burst and Japan entered its biggest recession since the late 1940s, a period in which economists came to characterize the nation as a 'dormant giant'. Contraction of the economy forced down wages and the price of goods but also made the yen gain value. A strong yen made Japan's exports less competitive and so the Bank of Japan began to exercise quantitative easing in an attempt to devalue the currency. Indeed, Japan was the first nation to use quantitative easing as a means of stimulating economic growth, pre-empting the response of several countries to the global financial crisis of 2008. In the aftermath of the 2008 crisis, the Bank of Japan purchased government bonds at up to sixty per cent of gross (or annual) domestic product, in effect doubling the amount of yen in circulation, and far exceeding the twenty-two per cent adopted by the US and the UK.

Faced with the rapid growth of currency markets in China and India, questions are continually asked whether the yen's mid-1990s zenith will ever be equalled. Yet it has survived more upheaval in its short history than most of the currencies in this book have over a much longer period. Furthermore, its relative stability ensures that it remains a 'safe-haven' currency, favoured by investors when there is uncertainty in the markets, and it is the third most widely traded currency. Its place amongst the 'best usages of the nations of the world', hoped for at its inception, would appear to be guaranteed for many years ahead.

The Pound

Life is pounds, shillings and pence.

The Mystery of Edwin Drood *by Charles Dickens (1812–70),*
published 1870.

THE POUND is some fifteen hundred years old and, like
many monetary terms, it was originally a weight measurement.
It comes from 'pondus', the Latin word for 'weight'. In the
Roman world weights were measured in 'libra' subdivided
into twelve 'unciae', hence the imperial weight standard which
abbreviates 'libra' to lbs and turns 'unciae' to ounces. The
£ symbol is merely a stylized and barred 'L' for 'libra'. Even
under the Romans this shifted across to have a monetary
role, with the Roman coins solidus and denarius related to an
original libra weight and leading eventually to the abbreviation
£sd for pounds, shillings and pence.

The pound emerged as a monetary term in the British Isles
in the centuries that followed the Roman withdrawal between
AD 407 and 411. The Romans' sophisticated currency system
had rapidly declined, to be followed by a period in which no
coins were made in Britain. From the early seventh century
the rulers of a group of coalescing kingdoms which are now
thought of as 'Anglo-Saxon' revived the idea of making coined
money. Their coins reflected the coinage in use on continental
Europe, especially in the Frankish lands (modern France and
western Germany), where coinage had continued unbroken
from the late Roman period. The first 'English' coins were
small gold pieces copying the standard Frankish tremissis:
these were probably known as 'shillings', a word that meant
'fragment' or 'section'. Dwindling stocks of gold led the Anglo-
Saxons at some point between the 660s and the 680s to replace
the gold coinage with an entirely new silver coinage, again

following what was happening in Frankia. These were the first local denarii, or pennies.

In the later eighth century the leading Anglo-Saxon king, Offa of Mercia (reigned 757–96), changed the style of these pennies to match those of his great Frankish contemporary Charlemagne (reigned 768–814). These silver pennies were to be made at a rate of 240 from the pound weight of silver. In England, as in other Germanic areas, the word pound ('pfund' among Germanic tribes and 'pund' in Old Norse) was adopted to describe 240 pennies rather than using a variation of 'libra' ('livre', 'lira'), which was what happened in Romance-speaking Europe. This system of 240 pennies to the pound, with the shilling as an intermediate unit of 12 pennies, survived unchanged until decimalization in 1971. Furthermore, since this emergence of the pound as a monetary unit worth 240 pennies, its existence has been a continuous one, without any revaluation. While there was a new penny introduced in 1971, there has never been a new pound; a longevity that is unique.

There are twenty shillings [scillingas] in a pound [punde], and twelve times twenty pence [penega] is a pound.

From the Enchiridion (manual) by Byrhtferth (about 970–1020), written 1011.

The medieval monetary system had no need for an actual coin that was worth as large a sum as a pound. Indeed, for centuries there was no larger denomination coin available than the penny. Before 1279 there was usually no smaller denomination available either: half and quarter pennies (farthings) were only obtainable by cutting up silver pennies. This was simply because the early medieval economy was not as monetized as today's economies. In 1087, for example, it is thought that only about 9 million sterling pennies, or 37,000 pounds, were in circulation throughout the whole of England. A common labourer probably earned about a penny a day, but lodging would have been provided as part of this and he would also have received a portion of his income in the form of food and drink. Nevertheless, reckoning in pounds was important to landowners who collected rent and taxes, and distributed wages to the people who worked for them. Gradually the population grew and economic and commercial life became more complex. Markets and fairs were established, cities and towns grew in size, and regional and international trade expanded greatly: England was gradually becoming monetized. By 1300, for example, the amount of money in circulation is estimated to have risen to between 1.1 million and 1.4 million pounds.

STERLING From the early twelfth century the silver pennies of the king of England were increasingly known by the rather mysterious word sterling. The word may have been derived from the Middle English root 'ster' which means 'strength' or 'stability' and, eventually, pound and sterling became interchangeable. It was important for medieval kings to maintain the quality of the coinage and, in 1124, Henry I (reigned 1100–35) publicly and very brutally demonstrated his commitment to sterling by calling his moneyers to an inquest about falling levels of silver in the coins. Dissatisfied with their explanations, Henry had two-thirds of them summarily castrated and their right hands chopped off.

An if my word be sterling yet in England.

The deposed king tries to reassert his authority in Richard II, set in the fourteenth century, by William Shakespeare (1564–1616), about 1595.

Increased monetization was not the only reason that the English kings began to introduce higher value coins, including coins made of gold. England's bullion had always been earned through foreign trade but there were problems with the supply of silver after about 1300 when Europe's mines became exhausted. English kings occasionally reduced the weight of the coins to stretch out the silver supply but they were averse to reducing its purity. In the meantime gold began to flow into western Europe mainly from Hungary and Africa. Beginning in Italy, the scarcity of silver had been mitigated by the reintroduction of gold coins, namely the florin, which also assisted larger-scale trade. England followed suit in 1344 by introducing its version of a double gold florin, valued at six shillings (seventy-two pennies). Partly because this coin was not divisible into the pound, its introduction was not successful and it was replaced in the same year by the noble, valued at six shillings and eight pence: a third of a pound or half an English mark. On this coin the king stands in a ship holding a sword and a shield. The noble became a trusted and popular coin for international trade and, similarly to the sterling penny, was sometimes imitated abroad. Eventually the noble was replaced by the angel as the coin worth a third of a pound, so-called because it featured the Archangel Michael fighting the devil, represented by a dragon.

The gradual introduction of these high-value gold coins meant that, by the 1460s, circulation of the coinage consisted of about two-thirds valued in gold against a third in silver, and in 1489 the first coin valued at a pound was introduced by Henry VII (reigned 1485–1509). It was actually called a sovereign, owing to the depiction of a full length portrait of the king. Perhaps more symbolic than practically useful, these magnificent coins probably emulated the large gold coins of Emperor Maximilian I (reigned 1486–1519), produced since 1487.

Over the centuries the weights of the English gold and silver coins had been reduced, generally in response to the changing value of the precious metals themselves, especially as the values of gold and silver shifted against each other. Medieval English kings, unlike some of their continental rivals, did not generally manipulate their coinage for profit. In the sixteenth century, however, a more dramatic change took place, as a result of the deliberate policy of Henry VIII (reigned 1509–47) and his advisors. Henry VIII was one of England's less financially responsible monarchs. He spent lavishly on his court and on military endeavours, serving to decimate the Royal treasury.

Gold sovereign of Henry VII minted in London, 1504–9. 14.90 g, diam. 41 mm.

Looking to the coinage for a quick financial win, he reduced the precious metal content of the coins, while expecting them to pass for the same value. The process intensified in 1544–51 during the so-called 'Great Debasement', leading to a great deal of confusion about the value of each coin. The debased coins dropped in value against better quality coins, which tended to fall out of use into hoards or move abroad: bad money drives out good, according to Gresham's Law. A debased penny meant the purchasing power of the pound fell in parallel and the value of older coins with more precious metal grew, in spite of their notional initial value. It was in this way that gold coins of different weights, and sometimes even of foreign origin, could circulate together, as long as everyone knew their value in £sd. Nevertheless, the high international reputation of the English coinage was damaged and it took over a decade for Henry's successors and their ministers to sort out the monetary chaos. In 1560–1 Elizabeth I (reigned 1558–1603) was finally able to purge the English currency of base coinage and restore a sound sterling currency. Most people suffered financially: 'bitter medicine', as the queen herself said.

Today it would seem inconceivable that the value of a modern pound coin could ever rise above a pound. But then, of course, a modern pound coin has almost no intrinsic value as bullion. This was not always the case and, in the sixteenth and seventeenth centuries, different versions of the pound appeared that were subsequently revalued upwards as the price of gold changed relative to silver. This included the old fine-gold sovereign introduced by Henry VII that was revalued at thirty shillings (ten shillings above a pound) by the later Tudors and James I (king of England, Wales and Scotland 1603–25). A crown-gold pound sovereign was added by Elizabeth, which James I subsequently renamed a 'unite' as part of his project to unite England and Scotland. After 1619 a new lighter pound coin was needed, in reaction to the changing relative value of gold and silver. The older coins survived but were revalued upwards to twenty-two shillings.

The new lighter gold pound, retained throughout the Civil War and Commonwealth periods, itself became misaligned with

CIVIL WAR After Charles I's (reigned 1625–49) last breach with Parliament in 1642 he was forced to leave London and subsequently lost control of the Mint, based at the Tower of London. To finance the war he established mints in Royalist strongholds around the country and made coins from bullion donated by his supporters. Between 1642 and 1644 Charles issued an enormous silver pound coin depicting the king on horseback after a design by the French engraver Nicholas Briot (about 1579–1646). A propaganda message was inscribed on the back abbreviating the king's 'Declaration', made in Wellington, Shropshire, in 1642, and promising to uphold the protestant religion, laws of England and the liberty of parliament.

Silver pound coin of Charles I minted in Oxford, 1643. 120.58 g, diam. 52mm.

gold prices and was revalued upwards. Thus yet another gold pound was introduced in 1662–3 and nicknamed the guinea, after the Guinea coast of West Africa, the main source of the bullion used in its production. The bullion was imported by the Royal African Company which had been established to explore and exploit the African continent for its wealth. The guineas produced from this bullion were stamped with the badge of the company in the form of an elephant. In the 1690s, however, there was a massive shift in gold prices, following the discovery of gold in Portuguese Brazil. The guinea was allowed to fluctuate in value against the silver-based money of account before eventually being stabilized at twenty-one shillings (252 pennies) in 1717. A five-guinea coin was also minted featuring the inscription 'DECVS ET TVTAMEN' on its edge, meaning 'a decoration and safeguard' (against the edges of the coin being clipped). The same inscription often appears on the edge of the modern pound coin.

The innate tensions in bimetallism (using two precious metals in one monetary system) continued to create problems for the pound into the eighteenth century, which intensified as money played a greater range of roles in people's lives. Furthermore, the government was generally indifferent to the challenge of supplying sufficient small change and the Mint also failed to balance the prices it offered for silver and gold, especially with the impact of the new Brazilian gold supplies. Silver was generally undervalued, leading merchants to export it to the continent where they could sell it for more. The East India Company alone exported silver valued at 5.7 million pounds between 1700 and 1717. A 1698 report by the Secretary to the Treasury had found that, of 3 million pounds in silver coins struck since 1663, almost none were still in circulation. In spite of a major re-coinage between 1696 and 1698, the price of silver still remained higher overseas. In the absence of silver, copper coins were gradually adopted for transactions of low value, while gold remained important for high-value payments. Of crucial significance was a 1717 report by Master of the Mint Sir Isaac Newton (1642–1727), who recommended that the pound move away from silver to a de facto gold standard. The result was that, by 1730, nine-tenths of all payments were made in gold.

Aside from the coinage, people were increasingly resorting to paper money in order to exchange their pounds. This was made possible by the establishment of a network of provincial banks from the late seventeenth century. According to the entries in his diary, Samuel Pepys (1633–1703) regularly instructed his banker to make payments on his behalf. In the 1700s Britain's banking network was largely presided over, in Scotland, by the Bank of Scotland and in England and Wales by the Bank of England. Both these banks issued notes that circulated alongside notes issued by provincial banks, with the bearer able to redeem their value in coin at any time. Often the Bank of England guaranteed the notes issued by the provincial banks with gold from its own reserve, typically maintained at about 8 million pounds. Today's Bank of England notes still feature the phrase 'I promise to pay the bearer on demand the sum of…' although the gesture is now more symbolic than real.

Ten pound note issued by the Northampton and Northamptonshire Bank, 1792. Banking crises were a relatively regular occurrence and this particular bank collapsed less than a year after issuing this note. 192 x 113 mm.

Paper pound notes had their disadvantages and were prone to overprinting. Furthermore, in times of uncertainty and panic, people favoured the physical reassurance of gold coins over paper currency. In 1797 a failed invasion of Wales by the French triggered a panic and a run on the gold reserve. The Bank of England had no option but to suspend the convertibility of its banknotes for gold. The government, faced with an acute shortage of coins, proceeded to coerce the Bank of England to print one-pound and two-pound notes on demand. James Gillray (1756 or 1757–1815) famously satirized this so-called period of 'Bank Restriction' by depicting the Bank as the 'Old Lady of Threadneedle Street' wearing a dress made of notes (see overleaf).

Having emerged victorious but financially battered from the Napoleonic Wars, the government formally put the pound on the gold standard. The Coinage Act of 1816 defined the pound's value against a specific weight in gold. The 'sterling silver' standard of ninety-two and a half per cent fine metal continued to be used until the twentieth century but the amount of silver no longer reflected the face value of the coin: monetary sterling was no longer silver based. The process of putting the pound on the gold

This print by James Gillray, 1797, shows the Old Lady of Threadneedle Street (the Bank of England) being seduced by the prime minister, William Pitt the Younger (1759–1806). The context of this satire was the government's coercion of the Bank of England to print notes, helping to finance war with France. 364 x 257 mm.

standard took six years to achieve since circulating pound notes had to be devalued to align with gold. The full convertibility of notes to coins was met with the introduction of a new sovereign coin, fixed to a pound in value. Its reverse depicted a design by Benedetto Pistrucci (1783–1855) featuring St George slaying the dragon. The coin would later become a symbol for the strength and might of Britain and by the late nineteenth century it was minted all over the Empire.

Gold pound sovereign of George III minted in London, 1818. 7.98 g, diam. 22 mm.

Periodic runs on the Bank of England's gold reserve in 1825, 1836 and 1839 forced the Bank to assess how it could regulate the pound's paper currency more effectively. In 1840 it proposed to separate its note-issuing department from its profiteering banking department. Its status as regulator was formalized by the Bank Charter Act in 1844 in which the Bank was granted monopoly over the issuing of notes by privately run banks. Thereafter the number of banks to whom licences were granted to print notes was greatly reduced.

The strength of the British economy and the ability of the Bank of England to regulate the currency engendered trust in the pound. From the 1850s London became a trading hub for international transactions. By 1870 more than sixty per cent of global trade was settled in pounds sterling while Britain's overseas investment, primarily in railways, banking and insurance, stood at 200 million pounds, increasing to 4 billion by the eve of the First World War.

The impact of the pound around the world was further increased by the rapid growth of the British Empire, especially after the 1880s, the height of the so-called 'scramble for Africa', when the sub-continent was carved up by rival European colonial powers. The pound was often introduced to regions where it was thought to provide greater monetary stability than existing currencies, regardless of the views of native populations on the subject. In pre-colonial Nigeria for example, cowrie shells, manillas and other wrought metal objects had circulated as currency, providing a perfectly serviceable medium of exchange for purchases within Nigeria's mainly agrarian economy. Yet they were deemed impractical by the British and an obstacle to economic interaction between the two countries. Sterling notes and coins were introduced in an attempt to drive out pre-colonial currencies, but in practice the two systems circulated side by side: as late as the 1950s, the price of a bride was still reckoned in cowries in some areas of south-east Nigeria.

Although a colonial single currency was seen as desirable by some British politicians and economists, it was never practically possible to implement. The Empire was disparate, and many countries already had stable currencies by the time they became

Pound note issued by the Bank of the Bahamas, 1930. The Latin motto below the ship on the left reads 'Pirates expelled, commerce restored', in reference to the Bahamas' 17th century reputation as a safe haven for pirates. The Bahamian pound remained pegged to sterling until 1966, when poor exchange rates prompted the island country to switch to the Bahamian dollar, tied to the US dollar. 151 x 84 mm.

British colonies. Instead, the Empire became broadly divided between three currency systems, based on the pound, rupee and dollar. In 1893 it was estimated that the total value of imports and exports for colonies using the pound stood at about 174 million pounds. By comparison, the total figure for British colonies using dollars or rupees stood at about 52 million pounds and 12 million pounds respectively.

A century of the pound's international dominance was disrupted by the outbreak of war in 1914. Military demands forced Britain to spend its financial assets abroad and to liquidate most of its gold reserves, forcing the pound off the gold standard in 1915. The recall of gold pound sovereigns had to be quickly compensated for by the printing of notes by the Treasury. They were nicknamed 'Bradburys' because they bore the signature of John Bradbury (1872–1950), secretary to the Treasury. In 1928 the passing of the Currency and Banknotes Act led to their replacement by Bank of England notes which, for the first time ever, were made fully legal tender. A new pound note was issued in the same year; the first Bank of England pound note in more than a century.

The exchange rate of the pound had been briefly pegged to the dollar in January 1916, but Britain's growing budget deficit forced it to abandon a fixed exchange rate after only a couple of months. At the end of the war a return to the gold standard was viewed by many countries as necessary for monetary stability, and a partial return was agreed in principle at a conference held in Genoa in 1922. The pound returned to the gold standard at pre-war parity in 1925 with a one-off issue of gold sovereigns, but with one crucial difference: notes could now only be redeemed for gold bullion, not coins. This partial gold standard would be ended by the Great Depression, and the pound abandoned it in 1931, a move that would immediately devalue it against those currencies which retained their gold backing. Conversely, its weak value provided a boost to exports and aided economic recovery. In the same year the pound briefly became the world's foremost reserve currency once more, accounting for about fifty per cent (compared to the dollar's forty per cent) of all world reserves.

During the Second World War Britain practised isolationist policies with its colonies, imposing trade controls to artificially prop up the value of the pound. The policy was only partly successful and, by the war's latter stages, the UK was almost bankrupt. At Bretton Woods in New Hampshire in 1944, a conference was held between the allied nations in an attempt to define what would become the post-war monetary system. The influential economist J.M. Keynes (1883–1946) was sent to negotiate on behalf of British interests. In return for much needed loans he effectively sacrificed the dominance of the pound by removing the restrictions on countries converting their sterling reserves to dollars. Almost immediately, residents of foreign countries flocked to the banks to change their weakened pounds to dollars. The results were disastrous and convertibility had to be suspended after just five weeks. Pound reserves in foreign banks would never increase again.

The Bretton Woods system fixed the exchange rate of the dollar at 4.03 for every pound, but Britain's slow economic recovery made it difficult for successive governments to maintain parity with the stronger dollar. The pound was devalued by more than thirty per cent to 2.80 dollars in 1949 with further crises ensuing in 1961 and almost continuously from 1964 to

1967, when it was devalued again. In an attempt to control inflation the government limited the exchange of pounds to other currencies and, from 1966 until 1979, tourists were prohibited from taking more than fifty pounds abroad. High inflation continued into the 1970s and significantly reduced the purchasing potential of the coins and notes in circulation. The problem was first addressed in 1982 with the introduction of a twenty-pence coin to alleviate demand for five-pence and ten-pence coins. In 1984 the halfpenny coin was withdrawn because it was now practically worthless.

The first coin to be known specifically as a pound was only introduced in 1983 when it replaced the Bank of England pound note. More than 443 million were minted in the year of their introduction. Made from nickel-brass, its size and golden hue provided a symbolic nod to the pound sovereigns that had circulated up until the collapse of the gold standard in 1915. The Royal Mint had in fact resumed production of gold pound sovereigns in 1957, albeit in the tens of thousands, rather than the millions that were minted before 1915. They remain legal tender but there is little point in spending them: their value as gold bullion (about 175 pounds at 2015 prices) far exceeds their nominal face value.

By the beginning of the twenty-first century the pound remained the currency of the United Kingdom as well as a number of former colonies and protectorates around the world. Sterling's share of world currency markets hovered at around twelve per cent, the fourth highest in the world. At the same time, politicians debated whether Britain should drop the pound and join the European single currency, but arguments were postponed by the euro crisis that erupted in the wake of global economic crisis in 2007–8.

In 2014 the pound became the subject of another debate regarding its sovereignty, this time in the vote for Scottish independence, held in September 2014. The British government suggested that an independent Scotland would have to give up the pound, while Scottish politicians argued that the pound was as much a part of their identity as it was for the rest of

DECIMALIZATION OF THE POUND In 1966 the British government announced that the pound would be decimalized, reducing the number of pennies in the pound from 240 to 100. In the process a number of denominations, including the crown and the florin, were dropped. A Decimal Currency Board was appointed to oversee the changeover and organized a public competition to appoint a designer for the new coins, which was won by Christopher Ironside (1913–92). Ironside's coins were introduced on 15 February 1971, known as 'D-Day', or 'Decimal Day'. The Decimal Currency Board produced

information posters and broadcast adverts on national television to familiarize a potentially sceptical British public with the pound's new structure.

If they give me my pension in this new money
I shall give it back to them: where it hurts!

A line from Granny Gets the Point, *a light-hearted ITV information film sponsored by the Decimal Currency Board, first broadcast in 1971.*

Christopher Ironside's designs for a pound coin, mid-1960s. The Government decided against introducing a pound coin during the re-coinage of 1971, and they were not introduced until 1983. In 2014 it was announced that it would be replaced by a new twelve sided pound coin, ostensibly to combat counterfeiting. 544 x 368 mm.

the United Kingdom. In a speech, George Osborne (1971–), Chancellor of the Exchequer said that 'as the SNP [Scottish National Party] says, it is Scotland's pound as much as the rest of the UK's. They are like the angry party to a messy divorce. But the pound isn't an asset to be divided up between two countries after a break-up as if it were a cd collection'. In the end, Scotland voted to remain in the UK and the currency question was averted. Nevertheless, these impassioned arguments had demonstrated, for a time, the continued relevance of the pound as a potent symbol of national identity.

The Dollar

*...the money unit of the United States, being by
the resolve of Congress of the 6th July, 1785,
a dollar, shall contain of fine silver, three
hundred and seventy-five grains, and sixty-four
hundredths of a grain.*

Report of the Board of the US Treasury, *1785*.

THE US DOLLAR, today the most widely used currency
across the globe, has in many ways carried on the legacy of
Spanish pieces of eight, the first global currency. Although
early settlers from England might have looked to continue the
use of sterling across the Atlantic this did not prove practicable.
The previous chapter mentioned how, in the seventeenth
century, the English government struggled with the challenge
of supplying small change. Facing an acute shortage of coins,
it was equally loath to export them to the recently established
colonies in the Americas. The early settlers were not particularly
wealthy and they took little cash with them on their passage
to the New World. Having insufficient coinage in sterling,
they at first resorted to commodity currency of the same type
being used by the native peoples. This included wampum, a
type of shell. The earliest known written record relating to its
use from Massachusetts, in 1637, ordered that it 'should passe
at 6 a penny for any sume under 12d'. Rice and tobacco also
passed as currency, but their use relied on maintenance of strict
quality controls. Furthermore, the desire for interchangeability
between these commodity currencies and coins led to the colonial
governments assigning the commodities fixed exchange rates or
prices in sterling. There was widespread rioting in 1682 over the
price of tobacco following a crop failure, because farmers were
prevented from increasing prices by the government.

Increasingly the settlers relied on imported coins, the most easily obtainable of which were made from Spanish silver, minted from bullion mined in Mexico and Bolivia. Amongst the most popular coins was the magnificent peso, strictly the 'peso da ocho reales', commonly known in English as 'pieces of eight'. The Spanish Empire, arguably the first global empire, minted millions of these coins over a period spanning four centuries. Foreign-exchange dealers in Europe had previously noted the similarity in their size and shape to those minted from silver mined in Bohemia at St Joachimsthal (modern Jáchymov, a spa town in the Czech Republic). The coins were called 'Joachimsthaler Guldengroschen', the latter term referring to a specific gold coin, against which the silver coins were valued. For convenience its name was quickly shortened to thaler. Henceforth thaler became the generic name for big silver coins and was translated into many languages, for example daler, daalder and tallero.

English speakers anglicized the word to dollar, applying the term to the big silver coins they tended to encounter, which were the Spanish pieces of eight. Their availability meant that they were often the most easily obtainable coins in regions that lacked the means to produce their own. They circulated in the West Indies and the American colonists exchanged them for dried fish, whale oil, pickled beef and grain. English laws prohibited colonists from trading with the Spanish and so most of the coins were smuggled into America, while some were spent by sailors on shore leave in American ports. They were imported into North America in huge numbers during the later eighteenth century, circulating widely in the thirteen British colonies as well as further north, in what would later become Canada.

Silver eight reales coin, a 'piece of eight', of Philip V minted in Spanish Mexico, 1732. It has been suggested that the banner wrapped around the pillar on the right could have inspired the $ sign. 27.13 g, diam. 39 mm.

Increasingly dissatisfied with British rule, the American colonists finally rebelled in 1776, throwing the monetary supply into crisis. Central to the revolutionaries' cause was their opposition to Stamp Tax which had been imposed by Britain in 1765. It would not have been politically expedient for the revolutionaries to finance their cause by raising taxes and an alternative solution had to be found. They resolved instead to issue IOUs in the form of paper continental bills which would circulate alongside paper bills already issued by a number of states. However the bills were traded at a confusing variety of prices and, since they were issued in large volumes and could not be converted into coins, widespread inflation ensued.

Currency reform became a priority and, in 1785, two years after revolutionary victory in the War of Independence, Congress passed a resolution to officially adopt the dollar as its currency. In his capacity as minister to France, Thomas Jefferson (1743–1826) had witnessed at first hand the advantages of the French decimal monetary system. He insisted that the dollar should be subdivided into hundredth parts and named this subdivision 'cent' in homage to French centime coins.

In the years immediately following little was accomplished toward producing the new coinage. A handful of states produced copper, silver and token coinages but state mints were prohibited by the United States Constitution that took effect in 1789. In January 1791 Alexander Hamilton (1755 or 1757–1804), appointed Secretary of the Treasury by President George Washington, submitted a series of recommendations in a document entitled *Report on the Establishment of a Mint*. Drawing inspiration from Sir Isaac Newton's earlier 1717 report on the English Royal Mint, Hamilton proposed that gold coins should be minted for large transactions and silver for smaller transactions. The report also stated that the new coinage should be uniform in size and silver content to help bring about the economic unity of the thirteen founding states. The creation of national unity was a major aim of the Founding Fathers, as reflected by the motto 'e pluribus unum', 'out of many, one', that features on the Great Seal of the United States. The design, which was drawn up in 1782, was added to the coinage after 1795. Hamilton's recommendations were enacted by the Coinage Act, passed by Congress on 2 April 1792, which established the US Mint and authorized its construction in the nation's then capital at Philadelphia.

In its initial months the US Mint produced only a few half, one and two cents in copper but production quickly increased until it could supply the needs of the nation, while the Spanish dollars which were still in circulation were weighed and silver dollars were produced of the same size and weight to facilitate public acceptance of the new currency. First appearing in 1794, these coins portrayed Robert Scot's design featuring Liberty on the front and a perched eagle on the back. Scot was Chief Engraver at the US Mint from

Silver dollar, minted in Philadelphia, 1795. 27.92 g, diam. 39 mm.

1793 until his death in 1823. Some 1,758 dollars were minted in the year of its introduction and regional newspaper articles were quick to discuss the merits of its appearance.

Some of the dollars now coining at the Mint of the United States have found their way to this town...[The] tout ensemble has a pleasing effect to a connoisseur; but the touches of the graver are too delicate and there is a want of that boldness of execution which is necessary to durability and currency.

New Hampshire Gazette, *December 1794.*

Spanish pieces of eight did not simply disappear after the introduction of the US silver dollar: many stayed in circulation, remaining legal tender in the US until 1857. They continued to provide a useful function around the world, not least in Australia where large numbers were imported in 1812 before having discs punched from their centres. Both disc and outer ring, known as 'holey dollars', then circulated separately as coins.

Pieces of eight also provided the model for trade dollars, produced by several countries in the nineteenth century for use in international commerce. Trade dollars circulated in many regions including China where they were treated as bullion, often acquiring chop marks when the purity of the silver was tested.

In the US the new government was keen to 'regulate the currency' and to achieve this (and to have a source of credit) it established the First Bank of the United States in 1791. However, the bank faced resistance from those who were opposed to an increase in federal power, and its twenty-year charter was allowed to expire in 1811. A second bank

Japanese silver trade dollar minted in Osaka, 1876, showing Chinese chop-marks. 27.20 g, diam. 39 mm.

followed in 1816, but it was later criticized by President Andrew Jackson (1767–1845), who thought that it was unconstitutional, favoured a legally privileged group of bankers at the expense of ordinary citizens, and had worsened trade fluctuations. The debate about renewing its charter between Jackson and Nicholas Biddle, the bank's president, dominated the 1832 presidential election. Jackson was re-elected and upheld his decision not to renew the bank's charter when it expired in 1836. In the absence of a national bank, state-chartered and privately owned banks were left to issue and regulate their own dollar notes, which are remarkable for their diversity and beautiful engravings. Following the rapid expansion of the economy, the number of private banks increased until there were almost 3,000 in operation by the outbreak of the American Civil War in 1861.

The Civil War of 1861–5 divided the country between the north and south and had a huge impact on the dollar. Both sides severed the link between coin and paper currency in order to print money freely for war expenditures, causing rampant inflation. Silver coins disappeared from circulation into hoards and exports. The Confederate south faced a monetary supply crisis since the Philadelphia Mint as well as most note engravers and paper producers were based in the Union-controlled north. To print notes some banks in the south resorted to less complex printing techniques such as lithography, while others stopped issuing notes altogether. In the absence of smaller denomination silver coins, many institutions and organizations such as insurance companies and local merchants were compelled to issue their own. In the north the Union government continued for a time to mint low-value silver coins, but many people hoarded or exported them as rising prices made the metal in them worth more than their purchasing power as legal tender.

In 1862 the Union government introduced a new legal tender bill that would become known as the 'greenback', owing to the use of green ink on its reverse. The decision to use green ink was initially practical, since it was found to stick to the paper better than other colours. The huge issue of irredeemable greenbacks drove them to a deep discount against the gold dollar. A year

United States one dollar legal tender note, the first 'greenback', issued 1862. The note depicts Salmon P. Chase, Secretary of the Treasury under Abraham Lincoln from 1861 to 1864. He introduced the motto 'In God We Trust' to the coinage. 300 million dollars in legal tender notes entered circulation in 1862 to help the government finance the costs of the Civil War, but they were not exchangeable for gold coins until 1879. 190 x 82 mm.

later it passed the National Banking Act, in which private banks were encouraged to apply for a federal charter, thereby becoming 'national banks'. The Act was aimed primarily at raising funds, but soon provided the basis for tighter regulation of the private banks, and resulted in a more uniform note currency than had previously existed.

Although the use of trade dollars remained prevalent beyond the United States, no other country officially adopted a dollar currency until British-ruled Canada became the first to do so in the 1850s. Canada was very familiar with the dollar, having previously used Spanish coins and also because it had developed close trade connections with its southern neighbour. It made economic sense to adopt a decimal dollar on a par with the US, and yet the British were reluctant to recognize dollars and cents alongside pounds, shillings and pence. This was partly owing to British fears that adoption of the US dollar would lead its Canadian provinces to break away. In 1858, the British capitulated and the Royal Mint was commissioned to produce silver cents. Dollar notes followed, although Canada's first circulating silver dollar coins were not struck until 1935, long after it had gained independence. Canada's larger-denomination banknotes were provided by its commercial banks until the Bank of Canada began operations in 1935.

Despite the rapid growth of the US economy in the last quarter of the nineteenth century, the dollar's share of world currency markets remained low. One reason for this stemmed from the instability of the US economy which, although powerful, suffered numerous crises and setbacks in the years preceding the First World War. After the end of the Civil War the government eventually restored the gold standard, but its commitment remained uncertain owing to the Free Silver movement. The Free Silver movement, driven by silver mining interests, argued that the dollar should be backed by both gold and silver, a bimetallic standard. Even when the dollar officially returned to the gold standard in 1879, the government offered a concession to the pro-silver lobby by minting silver dollars which were immediately stored in vaults, while silver certificates were printed to circulate in their place.

If they say bimetallism is good, but that we cannot have it until other nations help us, we reply that, instead of having a gold standard because England has, we will restore bimetallism, and then let England have bimetallism because the United States has it.

William Jennings Bryan, Democratic presidential candidate, 1896.

The Free Silver movement, led by William Jennings Bryan (1860–1925), Democratic candidate in the 1896 presidential campaign, argued that, for domestic purposes, a bimetallic standard would ensure fairer payments for farmers. However,

international trade contracts were more risky
if written out in a dollar that was backed
by either of two metals, given the age-old
fact that the relative price of the two
metals could vary. Bryan was defeated
in the 1896 election and in 1900 the
Gold Standard Act was passed, making
notes redeemable solely in gold. The Act
affirmed the US government's commitment
to the gold standard.

Inherent instabilities within the tightly regulated national
banking system were laid bare in 1907 by a crash in which
almost fifty per cent was wiped from the value of the New York
Stock Exchange. As a result of the crash the Republican senator
Nelson Aldrich (1841–1915) was appointed to head a new
National Monetary Commission to stabilize the US economy.
Aldrich's plan, subsequently modified and passed by Congress

Presidential campaign badge of William Jennings Bryan, 1896. Diam. 22 mm.

Gold $20 'double-eagle' coin, 1908, designed by the sculptor and medallist
Augustus Saint-Gaudens (1848–1907). The magnificent artistry of this piece,
which was minted up until the dollar left the gold standard in 1933, features
Liberty striding purposefully towards the dawn. The coin came to symbolize
the apogee of the US gold standard. 33.41 g, diam. 34 mm.

in 1913 as the Federal Reserve Act, oversaw the creation of the Federal Reserve. It eventually assumed control of note production (national banks continued to issue until the 1930s) and had the power to influence financial conditions by its lending and open market policies. It could also authorize national banks with capital reserves of at least a million dollars to establish branches in foreign countries. In the late 1800s there had been laws prohibiting US national banks from having international branches, although private banks such as J.P. Morgan and Brown Brothers & Co. were not subject to such restrictions. By 1920 US banks would have more than 180 branches abroad.

Besides banking reform, the early 1900s also witnessed a transformation in US foreign policy, where the government began to promise loans and financial advice to countries deemed to be politically unstable, but where the US had a commercial stake. Designed to be mutually beneficial, 'dollar diplomacy', as it was dubbed under the Taft administration (1909–13), had achieved success by peaceful means in the Dominican Republic in 1905. However, its critics argued that dollar diplomacy was primarily motivated by greed and self-interest. In Nicaragua, for example, President José Santos Zelaya (1853–1919), a leader with ambitions to unite Central America, had been a thorn in the side of US interests, in part because he proposed a rival canal to that being built by the US in Panama. By making loans to Zelaya's opponents, the US was largely responsible for his 1909 downfall. In Nicaragua and other Latin American nations, dollar diplomacy often led to military intervention to ensure that financial reforms were adopted and loan repayments were maintained. It led to accusations that it was merely a thinly veiled form of imperialism, and its unpopularity outside the US led to its eventual abandonment.

The outbreak of war in Europe in 1914 brought the US to the fore in the financial markets, and the disruption in the value of sterling swung financial business decisively away from London. Almost overnight, the US stepped up to become a creditor nation, with New York banks recycling an influx of gold deposits from Europe by extending dollar loans abroad. The influx allowed the

Federal Reserve to maintain the gold standard throughout the war. After the war, the US made out loans which were, of course, denominated in dollars to aid post-war European reconstruction, and there was a rise in demand for US consumer goods. From the mid to late 1920s the dollar, now the most stable currency in the world, became a leading reserve currency.

The late 1920s boom, which had peaked in mid-1929, came to a sudden end with the catastrophic collapse of the New York Stock Exchange. The ensuing Depression caused numerous rural US banking failures, and at the peak of the crisis between August 1931 and January 1932, 1,860 US banks were wiped out. The US initially attempted to defend the gold standard, maintaining the gold backing of the dollar at forty per cent of circulating notes. However, the Federal Reserve Board failed to offset the contraction of the monetary supply brought on by bank runs. In April 1933 President Franklin D. Roosevelt (1882–1945) took the dollar off the gold standard through a series of executive orders. In 1934, the Gold Reserve Act was passed nationalizing all gold, compelling the Federal Reserve to turn over all gold bullion coins and certificates to the Treasury. In a bid to make exports more competitive and to halt deflation, the Act also increased the price of gold from 20.67 dollars to 35 dollars an ounce. This devalued the dollar by more than a third.

The collapse of the international gold standard and continuing global downturn had far reaching consequences for the dollar. Gold coins were gone, while tighter monetary regulation, including the end of the national bank note system in 1935, curtailed a number of note types. There were widespread monetary shortages, prompting a revival of the sort of localism that had been prevalent during the Civil War, with so-called 'Depression scrip', or token money being issued by businesses across the country. Amid banking failures, widespread unemployment and poverty, Depression-era literature became increasingly preoccupied with the plight of the displaced and the dispossessed. Among those who suffered most were farming communities forced to leave the American mid-west, where the effects of the Depression had been exacerbated by drought and crop failure.

Tom swallowed the last of his bread. 'Got any more, Ma?' 'No,' she said. 'That's all. You made a dollar an' that's a dollar's worth.'

Tom Joad goes hungry in The Grapes of Wrath by John Steinbeck (1902–68), published 1939 and describing refugee farmers fleeing the 'Okie' dustbowl in the 1930s.

The US economy did not fully recover from the effects of the Great Depression until after the Second World War. Britain and its allies had to use their dollar reserves to procure goods and materials from the US and, as these reserves became exhausted, the US began to extend substantial loans to the allies. At the end of the war the US initiated a four-year programme to aid European economic recovery, known unofficially as the Marshall Plan, which was essentially a lump sum payment in dollars. It cost the US an estimated ten per cent of its annual budget, but the money could be used to buy back US goods, supporting manufacturing and ensuring that recipient nations did not resort to trade isolation and barter.

The meeting at Bretton Woods in 1944 resulted in favour of US economic predominance and established the dollar as the principal reserve currency for other countries, with the dollar backed by gold. The Bretton Woods system was monitored by the newly created International Monetary Fund (IMF). It flooded world currency markets with dollars, but exposed US gold reserves to the danger that central banks could cash in their reserves. This danger increased after 1960, when the value of dollar assets in foreign central reserves began to exceed the value of gold in the US Treasury. Gold was a finite resource, whereas dollars could be printed on demand. The problem faced by the Treasury and the Federal Reserve was that expanding the dollar supply would improve the government's fiscal position, but an unlimited supply would result in inflation and undermine the US commitment to the direct convertibility of dollars for gold.

In 1961 the US and seven European countries agreed to pool their gold reserves in a bid to collectively protect their respective currencies. The US provided fifty per cent of the gold and, for a couple of years the system successfully defended its price, fixed since 1934 at 35 dollars an ounce. However, a gold famine in 1965 meant that the gold pool found it increasingly difficult to keep prices stable. In November 1967 a run on sterling forced the UK government to devalue its currency by fourteen per cent. The pool responded by selling off gold worth a billion dollars and another billion in December 1967 in a bid to stabilize the market. The selloff could not be sustained and, in March 1968, the London gold market was closed down. At an emergency meeting a two-tier pricing system was agreed in which the price of gold was allowed to fluctuate unofficially, while still being fixed at 35 dollars an ounce. This complicated system opened up the possibility that a central bank could buy up cheap US gold and sell it for a higher price on the open market. The result would be a flooding of the market with dollars, devaluation of the currency and the collapse of the US balance of trade.

For a time, threats against NATO-member governments not to redeem their dollars prevented this from occurring, yet the reaction of the Nixon administration to a potential run in 1971 was indicative of the fragility of the system. In May 1971 Senator John Connally (1917–93), Secretary of the Treasury, gave a speech threatening European countries with higher export tariffs if they sold off their dollar reserves. The bullying tactic backfired and European bankers, objecting to Connally's tone, accelerated their conversion of dollars to gold. In August 1971 Britain tried to cash in a proportion of its dollar reserves and the US Treasury, faced with no alternative, suspended dollar to gold convertibility. With the price of gold no longer fixed against the dollar, it escalated to unprecedented levels, reaching 850 dollars an ounce by the 1980s.

The suspension of dollar to gold convertibility was presented by President Richard Nixon (1913–94) as part of his 'New Economic Program', but is perhaps better known as the 'Nixon Shock'. Broadly isolationist in tone, it placed a temporary ten per cent surcharge on imports to protect US production. With an election looming in 1972, Nixon coerced the Federal Reserve Board to increase the monetary supply, resulting in inflation of the dollar. Another run on the dollar in 1973 ended the fixed exchange-rate system that was supposed to replace Bretton Woods, and led commentators to question if the dollar was too unstable to remain a viable reserve currency. However and, against expectation, the dollar survived the crisis and increased its share of the reserve currency market throughout the decade, in part because there was no realistic alternative.

By 1977 eighty per cent of foreign exchange reserves were held in dollar assets. This caused Michael Blumenthal (1926–), Secretary of the Treasury, to make an ill-timed remark that the dollar was over strong, resulting in a mini-run on the currency. In 1979 Saudi Arabia and other major oil producing countries hinted that they would like to switch their reserves away from dollars, but there seemed to be few viable alternatives. Fearing inflation, the Bundesbank, for example, actively discouraged Iran, a country in the throes of a violent revolution, from buying into the Deutsche mark. Iran nevertheless liquidated its dollar reserves, but it was the only country to do so.

The US Government averted potential crisis by tightening monetary policy to fight inflation, strengthening the dollar and, from the mid-1980s it entered a period of stability. Indeed, entering the twenty-first century, it would take a crisis of monumental proportions to shake international belief in the dollar.

CONTROLLING COUNTERFEIT PRODUCTION In 2012 it was calculated that seventy-three per cent of all US dollar bills were in circulation outside of the United States of America. The proliferation of dollars across the globe has created huge practical problems for the US Treasury as it tries to limit the production of counterfeits. Notes are rarely returned to the Treasury once they have left the US, which makes it difficult for the government to assess the number of fakes. In the first decade of the twenty-first century the US government accused North Korea of state-sanctioned forgery owing to the appearance of good quality counterfeit 100 dollar Federal Reserve notes, known as 'superdollars'.

Counterfeit US 100 dollar bill, dated 1974. Its French over-stamp suggests that it was circulating somewhere outside the US when it was discovered to be fake. It is somewhat ironic that a portrait of Benjamin Franklin (1706–90) should feature on a counterfeit note, since his pioneering methods in developing new printing techniques in the 1750s helped combat note forgery. 155 x 66 mm.

The 2007–8 banking crisis triggered by the collapse of the US housing market frightened private investors away from the dollar. Meanwhile the US budget deficit had swollen owing to protracted and costly wars in Afghanistan and Iraq, controversial tax cuts by the government and the crippling effects of global economic downturn. Its status as the international reserve currency of choice was being challenged by the fact that the US had entered its biggest recession since the 1930s. Surprisingly, however, central banks across the world responded to the crisis by stockpiling dollars. This was intended to safeguard against the volatile flow of capital investments, thus ensuring that nations could still satisfy their short-term foreign liabilities. South Korea,

Dollar bill, 2003. The design of the note, featuring George Washington, has remained unchanged since 1963 and recalls elements from 1860s Civil War issue notes. 155 x 65mm.

for example, increased its foreign currency reserves, primarily held in dollars, from five to twenty-five per cent of its gross domestic product. In 2012 sixty-one per cent of all currency reserves were held in dollars and there remained more than fifty countries whose currencies were pegged to the dollar exchange rate.

America's founding fathers could never have predicted that the dollar would become as ubiquitous, or indeed as vital to global economics in the twenty-first century. Today almost forty countries around the world issue a dollar currency in one form or another, some independent, and others pegged to the US dollar. It is a popular choice for new currencies, in part because countries wish to emulate the successful US currency model, but also owing to the enduring legacy of Spanish pieces of eight, the first global currency.

Conclusion

All things which can be exchanged need to be compared.
For this purpose coinage came into being... Money is
in fact a kind of measure which, by making things
measurable, reduces them to equality.

Aristotle (384–322 BC).

THE DOLLAR concludes this look at the history of money
through the stories of ten coins, considered as physical objects,
as economic players and as symbols of power. There are, of
course, stories that could be told about all monetary terms, how
they originated, what roles they performed, how they spread,
survived for centuries, and how their appearance and meaning
evolved. Those featured in this book span the history of money,
from survivors of the ancient world to the currency giants of
the twenty-first century. They help to illustrate broad themes
like the characteristics of empires, trade, migration and the
personalities of rulers.

The money discussed in the preceding chapters was issued
not just by rulers and governments, but also by banks, cities,
guilds, merchants and religious institutions. These all shared
a common purpose, an inherent conservatism that informed
their use of terminology and choice of designs, resulting in
the re-use and reinterpretation of iconic imagery. Even if
the currency suffered a catastrophic collapse or if broader
economic pressures created a need for reform, issuers have
tended to prefer continuity to radical change. This continuity
is often indicative of broader efforts to facilitate trade or
to promote a common political identity in regions that are
otherwise divided. A sudden change to the name or design
of the currency is often symbolic in itself, a result of political
revolution or economic strife.

*... all the absurd varieties of money that exist today,
with their effigies of princes, those symbols of misery.*

Victor Hugo (1802–85), 1855.

Four of the currencies featured in this book, the mark, florin (by
way of the guilder), drachma and several incarnations of the
franc, came to an end with the adoption of the euro. A currency
union such as the euro could be viewed as the final evolutionary
stage for the development of monetary terminology. Reflecting
on this union in 2002, Wim Duisenberg (1935–2005), president
of the European Central Bank, went as far as to say that the
euro was the first currency to have 'not only severed its link to
gold, but also its link to the nation-state'. By its very nature,
currency union includes regions that are otherwise politically,
culturally and economically independent. Nevertheless, as the
introduction to this book demonstrated, the euro is ultimately
a brand whose value has to be promoted and maintained, just
like those currencies it replaced. In this respect the way in which
terminology is employed is no different to any other currency.

*Gold circulates because it has value, whereas paper
has value because it circulates.*

Karl Marx (1818–83), 1859.

The ten monetary terms discussed here have endured
tremendous upheaval in their histories, especially in the
twentieth century as a result of changes to the physical form of
money. For some two and a half thousand years the monetary
supply remained broadly the same. The shekel and drachma
adopted the use of weighed pieces of silver as units of account
and, from then until the collapse of the international gold
standard in the 1930s, the value of currencies all over the
world was usually measured in relation to a precious metal.
Today's world currencies are divorced from the price of bullion
and there is no gold, silver or bimetallic standard. The global
economy has completely altered the way in which people

interact with money, and monetary terminologies have been pushed far beyond regional and national boundaries.

Furthermore, technological advances have meant that money no longer even needs to be physically tangible, but can instead consist of an encrypted digit. In 1994 *The Economist* said 'it is possible to imagine the development of e-cash reaching [a] final evolutionary stage…in which convertibility into legal tender ceases to be a condition for electronic money; and electronic money will thereby become indistinguishable from – because it will be the same as – other, more traditional sorts of money.' Its remarks were prescient, because the invention and rapid expansion of the internet from the mid-1990s removed many boundaries, both physical and ideological. It opened the world to the possibility that there could be decentralized, de-territorialized and wholly digital mediums of exchange that operate separately to traditional state-backed or state-controlled currencies. Many experiments at creating such peer-to-peer mediums of exchange have failed, with Bitcoin, invented in 2009, the most successful to date. Yet there remain significant barriers to the development of digital mediums of exchange. In order to provide a viable alternative to state-backed currencies, they often have to rely on marketing and use of incentives to promote their investment potential, and any form of digital payment needs significant infrastructure.

Multinational credit and debit card companies regularly forecast the so-called 'cashless revolution', the imminent demise of cash payments. In the early 1960s, Diners Club advertised its credit cards using the phrase 'Cash Died Today', while in the 2000s, Maestro advertised using the slogan 'Coins Get Lost'. Forty years apart, but the messages remain almost the same, perhaps suggesting that the prediction still remains somewhat premature. In the developing world especially, and despite the growth of mobile-phone banking, cash seems likely to remain the primary source of exchange and an important store of wealth for those without access to regular banking. The implication of all of this is that cash seems likely to remain the primary means by which different currencies, and the exchange systems they embody, continue to circulate.

If it ever happens, the end of cash will not automatically result in the end of named currencies. After all, people will still need to find a mutually accepted and trusted means by which to facilitate trade and exchange. The story of the shekel, among others, serves as a reminder that a name can both predate, and survive independently of, physical money. This versatility will ensure that an understanding of what lies behind monetary terms will continue to provide a window into broader themes in history.

Bibliography

Shekel

R. Abdy and A. Dowler, *Coins and the Bible* (London, 2013)

J. Liver, 'The half-shekel offering in biblical and post-biblical literature', *Harvard Theological Review*, 56:3 (1963), pp. 173–98

J.N. Postgate, *Early Mesopotamia: society and economy at the dawn of history* (London, 1992)

Y. Ronen, 'The enigma of the shekel weights of the Judean kingdom', *Biblical Archaeologist*, 59:2 (1996), pp. 122–5

Drachma

I. Carradice, *Greek coins* (London, 1995)

M. Dritsas, 'Monetary modernisation in Greece: bimetallism or the gold standard (1833–1920)', *Journal of European Economic History*, 28:1 (1999), p. 28

D. Evgenidou (ed.), *How much does it cost…our daily bread from ancient to modern times* (Athens, 2007)

G.K. Jenkins, *Ancient Greek coins* (London, 1972)

S. Lazaretou, 'Monetary and fiscal policies in Greece: 1833–1914', *Journal of European Economic History*, 22:2 (1993), p. 22

S. Lazaretou, 'Macroeconomic policies and nominal exchange rate regimes: Greece in the interwar period', *Journal of European Economic History*, 25:3 (1996), pp. 647–70

G.C. Logio, 'Greece in difficulties', *Contemporary Review* (July 1953), p. 184

G.E. Makinen, 'The Greek hyperinflation and stabilization of 1943–1946', *Journal of Economic History*, 46:3 (1986), pp. 795–805

J.G. Milne, 'The currency of Egypt under the Ptolemies', *Journal of Egyptian Archaeology*, 24:2 (1938), pp. 200–7

Denarius

J. Andreau, *Banking and business in the Roman world* (Cambridge, 1999)

A.M. Burnett, *Coinage in the Roman world* (London, 1991)

M.H. Crawford, *Coinage and money under the Roman Republic* (London, 1985)

R. Duncan-Jones, *Money and government in the Roman Empire* (Cambridge, 1998)

A.H.M. Jones, 'Inflation under the Roman Empire', *Economic History Review*, New Series, 5:3 (1953), pp. 293–318

J. Melville Jones, *A dictionary of ancient Roman coins* (London, 1990)

J.G. Milne, 'Roman coinage in Egypt in relation to the native economy', *Aegyptus*, 32:1 (1952), pp. 143–151

R. Reece, *The coinage of Roman Britain* (Stroud, 2002)

Florin

Dante Alighieri, trans. A.S. Kline, *The divine comedy* (Ann Arbor, 2004)

C.P. Barclay, 'The origins of the Godless Florin', *The Yorkshire Philosophical Society, annual report for the year 1991* (1991), pp. 51–61

C.M. Cipolla, *Money in sixteenth-century Florence* (London, 1989)

P. Grierson, 'The origins of the grosso and of gold coinage in Italy', *Numismatický Sbornik*, 12 (1971–2), pp. 33–44; reprinted in P. Grierson, *Later medieval numismatics (11ᵗʰ–16ᵗʰ centuries)*, Variorum Reprints (London, 1979)

Franc

A. Dowle and A. de Clermont, *Monnaies modernes, 1789 á nos jours* (Fribourg, 1972)

M. Flandreau, translated by O. Leeming, *The glitter of gold: France, bimetallism, and the emergence of the international gold standard, 1848–1873* (Oxford, 2004)

V. Hugo, *Les Misérables* (1862, English reprint London, 1982)

J. Lafaurie, *Les assignats et les papiers monnaies émis par l'état au XVIIIe siècle* (Paris, 1981)

N.J. Mayhew, *Coinage in France from the Dark Ages to Napoleon* (London, 1988)

M. Obstfeld and A.M. Taylor, 'Sovereign risk, credibility and the gold standard: 1870–1913 versus 1925–31', *Economic Journal*, 113:487 (2003), pp. 241–75

E.W. O'Neill Jr, 'French coinage in history and literature', *French Review*, 39:1 (1965), pp. 1–14

F.C. Spooner, *The international economy and monetary movements in France, 1493–1725* (Harvard, 1972)

Mark

R.A. Banyai, *The legal and military aspects of German money, banking, and finance 1938–1948* (Phoenix, 1971)

M.A. Denzel, *Handbook of world exchange rates, 1590–1914* (Farnham, 2010)

Deutsche Bundesbank (ed.), *Fifty years of the Deutsche mark: central bank and the currency in Germany since 1948* (Oxford, 1999)

W. Guttmann and P. Meehan, *The great inflation: Germany, 1919–1923* (Westmead, 1975)

D. Marsh, *The euro: the politics of the new global currency* (New Haven and London, 2009)

J. Pedersen and K. Laursen, *German inflation 1918–1923* (Amsterdam, 1964)

A. Ritschl, 'Review: Fifty years of the Deutshe mark: central bank and the currency in Germany since 1948, by Deutsche Bundesbank', *Journal of Economic History*, 61:1 (2001), pp. 198–9

B. Sprenger, *Das geld der Deutschen* (Paderborn, 2007)

R.H. Tilly, 'On the history of German monetary union', in P.L. Cottrell, G. Notaras and G. Tortella (eds), *From the Athenian tetradrachm to the euro: studies in European monetary integration* (Aldershot, 2007)

B. Widdig, *Culture and inflation in Weimar Germany* (London, 2001)

Rupee

R. Cribb, 'Political dimensions of the currency question 1945–1947', *Indonesia*, 31 (1981), pp. 113–36

P.L. Gupta, *Paper money in India* (Mumbai, 2000)

F.C. Harrison, 'An attempt to estimate the circulation of the rupee', *Economic Journal*, 1:4 (1891), pp. 721–51

L. James, *Raj: the making and unmaking of British India* (London, 1998)

W.H. Moreland, 'Sher Shah's revenue system', *Journal of the Royal Asiatic Society of Great Britain and Ireland*, 3 (1926), pp. 447–59

W. Mwangi, 'Of coins and conquest: the East African Currency Board, the Rupee Crisis, and the problem of colonialism in the East African Protectorate', *Comparative Studies in Society and History*, 43:4 (2001), pp. 763–87

J.F. Richards, *The Mughal Empire: the new Cambridge history of India* (Cambridge, 1993)

T. Roy, *India in the world economy: from antiquity to the present* (Cambridge, 2012)

B.R. Tomlinson, 'Britain and the Indian currency crisis, 1930-2', *Economic History Review*, New Series, 32:1 (1979), pp. 88–99

P.R. Thompson, *The East India Company and its coins* (Honiton, 2010)

Yen

A. Gordon, *A modern history of Japan: from Tokugawa times to the present* (Oxford, 2009)

K. Haitani, 'Japan's trade problem and the yen', *Asian Survey*, 13:8 (1973), pp. 723–39

W.J. Macpherson, *The economic development of Japan 1868–1941* (Cambridge, 1987)

M. Masayoshi, *Report on the adoption of the gold standard in Japan* (Tokyo, 1899)

M. Metzler, *Lever of empire: the international gold standard and the crisis of liberalism in prewar Japan* (London, 2006)

N.G. Munro, *Coins of Japan* (Yokohama, 1904)

M. Schiltz, *The money doctors from Japan: finance, imperialism and the building of the Yen Bloc 1895–1937* (London, 2012)

E. Scolinos, 'Japan: coming to terms with internationalization', *Asian Affairs*, 15:2 (1988), pp. 91–104

H. Shinjō, *History of the yen: 100 years of Japanese money-economy* (Kōbe, 1962)

T. Tsukamoto, *The old and new coins of Japan* (Tokyo, 1930)

L. Turner, 'A yen to trade', *The World Today*, 63:4 (2007), pp. 14–15

W.T. Ziemba and S.L. Schwartz, 'The growth in the Japanese stock market, 1949–90 and prospects for the future', *Managerial and Decision Economics*, 12:2 (1991), pp. 183–95

Pound

M. Allen, 'The volume of the English currency, 1158–1470', *Economic History Review*, New Series, 54:4 (2001), pp. 595–611

D. Blaazer, '"Devalued and dejected Britons": The pound in public discourse in the mid-1960s', *History Workshop Journal*, 47 (1999), pp. 121–40

G.L.M. Clauson, 'The British colonial currency system', *Economic Journal*, 54:213 (1944), pp. 1–25

N. Harris, 'The British and the euro', *Economic and Political Weekly*, 37:7 (2002), pp. 619–20

G. Krozewski, 'Sterling, the "minor" territories, and the end of formal empire, 1939–1958', *Economic History Review*, New Series, 46:2 (1993), pp. 239–65

N. Mayhew, *Sterling: the rise and fall of a currency* (London, 1999)

W.I. Ofonagoro, 'From traditional to British currency in southern Nigeria: analysis of a currency revolution, 1880–1948', *Journal of Economic History*, 39:3 (1979), pp. 623–54

G. Schmidt, 'The Latin element in the English currency system', *Journal of the Warburg and Courtauld Institutes*, 3:3/4 (1940), pp. 251–4

Spink & Sons, *Coins of England and the United Kingdom* (London, 1929, 49th edition 2014)

J.I. Walsh, 'How and why Britain might join the single currency: the role of policy failure', *Review of International Political Economy*, 14:5 (2007), pp. 868–92

Dollar

B. Bernanke, *Essays on the Great Depression* (Princeton, 2004)

A.S. Blinder, 'The role of the dollar as an international currency', *Eastern Economic Journal*, 22:2 (1996), pp. 127–36

R. Doty, *America's money–America's story* (Iola, 1998)

B. Eichengreen, *Exorbitant privilege: the rise and fall of the dollar and the future of the international monetary system* (Oxford, 2011)

J. Goodwin, *Greenback: the almighty dollar and the invention of America* (New York, 2003)

F. Heldring, 'Can the US dollar survive as a world reserve currency?', *Annals of the American Academy of Political and Social Science*, 500 (1988), pp. 23–32

D.G. Munro, 'Dollar diplomacy in Nicaragua, 1909–1913', *Hispanic American Historical Review*, 38:2 (1958), pp. 209–34

E.P. Newman and R.G. Doty (eds), *Studies on money in early America* (New York, 1976)

E.S. Rosenberg, 'Twenties/twenties hindsight', *Foreign Policy*, 120 (2000), pp. 84–5

E.S. Rosenberg, *Financial missionaries to the world: the politics and culture of dollar diplomacy 1900–1930* (Durham, 2003)

General

C.M. Cipolla, *Money, prices and civilization in the Mediterranean world* (Princeton, 1956)

B.J. Cohen, *The geography of money* (New York, 1998)

B.J. Cohen, 'Electronic money: new day or false dawn?', *Review of International Political Economy*, 8:2 (2001), pp. 197–225

P.L. Cottrell, G. Notaras and G. Tortella (eds), *From the Athenian tetradrachm to the euro: studies in European monetary integration* (Aldershot, 2007)

J. Cribb, B. Cook and I. Carradice, *The coin atlas: a comprehensive view of the coins of the world throughout history* (London 1990, 2003)

C. Eagleton and J. Williams (eds), *Money: a history* (London, 1997, second edition 2007)

'Electronic money: so much for the cashless society', *The Economist*, 26 November 1994, pp. 21–3

B. Eichengreen, *Globalizing capital: a history of the international monetary system* (Princeton, 1996)

European Central Bank, *How the euro became our money: a short history of the euro banknote and coins* (Frankfurt, 2007)

J. Grahl, *After Maastricht: a guide to European monetary union* (London, 1997)

P. Grierson, *The coins of medieval Europe* (London, 1991)

C. Howgego, *Ancient history from coins* (London, 1995)

F. Hutchinson, M. Mellor and W. Olsen, *The politics of money: towards sustainability and economic democracy* (London, 2002)

G. Ingham, *The nature of money* (Cambridge, 2004)

S. Lotz and G. Rocheteau, 'On the launching of a new currency', *Journal of Money, Credit and Banking*, 34:3:1 (2002), pp. 563–88

W.E. Metcalf (ed.), *The Oxford handbook of Greek and Roman coinage* (Oxford, 2012)

R. Mundell, 'A theory of optimum currency areas', *American Economic Review*, 51 (1961), pp. 657–65

H. Rey, 'International trade and currency exchange', *Review of Economic Studies*, 68:2 (2001), pp. 443–64

M. Shell, *The economy of literature* (London, 1978)

M. Shell, *Money, language, and thought* (London, 1982)

P. Spufford, *Money and its use in medieval Europe* (Cambridge, 1988)

Picture Credits

Except where otherwise stated, photographs in this book are © The Trustees of the British Museum, courtesy of the Department of Photography and Imaging. British Museum registration numbers are listed below. Further information about the Museum and its collection can be found at britishmuseum.org.

2	1935,0401.817	73	1984,0605.2226
4–5	1913,0909.1	75	G3,GERM.2110
6	1843,0116.170	76	SSB,75.170.2
9	2005,0607.1	77	1874,0605.2
16	1868,1228.33	79	1980,0378.85
17	TC,p242.5.Pop	80	1961,0609.127
18	1962,0408.1	81	© Library of Congress, Prints & Photographs Division, FSA/OWI Collection, LC-USE6- D-009361 [P&P]
20	D,7.94		
21	1927,1219.1		
25	G.3183; RPK,p32D.12. Ath; 1949,0411.447; 1920,0805.328; 1949,0411.407; 1842,1017.8; 1920,0805.354; 1846,0910.98	85	1996,1024.24
		89	1911,0709.2318
		93 above	1922,0522.15
		93 below	SSB,159.49
		96	1913,0909.1
26	© John Williams and Kevin Lovelock	99 above	2007,4137.13
29	1841,0726.288	99 below	1997,1036.2
31	1912,1007.7	103	1947,0604.3
32	1987,0648.1	104	1892,1001.2
33	1863,0728.1	105	Courtesy of the editor
36 above	1931,0611.24	107	1948,0908.4
36 below	1980,0378.417	108	1984,0605.8753
37	2008,4139.19	109	1935,0401.12714
39	1860,0328.230	114	1998,1104.62
42	R.7685	119	1935,0401.817
43	1843,0116.170	121	E.898
44	1860,0328.124	123	CIB.3339
48	1998,0401.1	124 above	J,3.68
51	1857,0901.192	124 below	1855,0321.14
52	1885,0405.35	126	1994,0915.776
55	1935,0401.5878	129	2006,0601.470 © Trustees of the British Museum/Crown Copyright
56 above	1895,0915.4		
56 below	1877,0502.2	131	1870,0408.1
61	1994,0915.776	133	C.3848
63	1850,0326.139	134	1976,0114.1047
65	E1956,0409.56	136	1984,0605.1616
66	1980,1213.29	138 above	2011,4140.1
67	1935,0401.10633	138 below	1964,1203.2
70	1906,1103.8337	144	2008,4168.121
71	2006,0405.357	145	2005,0808.1
72 above	1945,0404.2		
72 below	2009,4016.66		

Index